Stories for Circle Time and Assembly

Circle time creates a special time in the school week, when children can use a safe environment in which to think about their relationships, their behaviour and be honest about their problems and feelings.

This book provides a range of lively and engrossing stories for use in circle time activities, which are specially written to encourage the cognitive and emotional development of young children.

The author cleverly links twelve key value-based themes in the circle time stories which will stimulate discussion and enhance pupils' literacy skills and citizenship education. The stories in this book will:

- promote pupils' self confidence
- develop their interpersonal skills
- encourage active and responsible participation
- support deeper reflection
- enhance their literacy hour activities.

As well as circle time activity, this indispensable book also offers poems and suggested songs that can be used as the basis for a school assembly. Over-stretched KS1 & 2 teachers will find the stories and learning activities time-saving in their clarity and highly enjoyable to deliver.

Mal Leicester is professor emeritus at Nottingham University, based in the School of Education.

Stories for Circle Time and Assembly

Developing literacy skills and classroom values

Mal Leicester

 Routledge
Taylor & Francis Group

LONDON AND NEW YORK

First published 2006
by Routledge
2 Park Square, Milton Park, Abingdon, Oxon OX14 4RN

Simultaneously published in the USA and Canada
by Routledge
270 Madison Ave, New York, NY10016

Routledge is an imprint of the Taylor & Francis Group

© 2006 Mal Leicester

Typeset in Times New Roman by RefineCatch Limited, Bungay, Suffolk
Printed and bound in Great Britain by TJ International Ltd, Padstow, Cornwall

British Library Cataloguing in Publication Data
A catalogue record for this book is available from the British Library

Library of Congress Cataloging-in-Publication Data
A catalog record for this book has been requested

ISBN10: 0–415–35535–4
ISBN13: 978–0–415–35535–3

Contents

Acknowledgements

As always, I am grateful to Karen Langley for helping me to prepare the manuscript. I am also grateful to Roger Twelvetrees for invaluable assistance and advice in the final stages of the work. I want to thank postgraduate students at Nottingham Trent University for helpful comments on some of the stories. In particular I am very grateful to Anne McDonnell for her perceptive advice about both the stories and the learning activities in relation to the education of children at Key Stages One and Two.

Mal Leicester

Introduction

Stories, Circle Time, Literacy and Assemblies

This is the third book in which I have used the power of story as a gateway to important areas of the curriculum. The first book (*Stories for Classroom and Assembly*) focuses on values education (personal, social, moral, emotional, spiritual). The second (*Stories for Inclusive Schools*) explores the issue of "difference", tackling bullying and prejudice head-on. In this book, ten **new** themed stories link **Circle Time** and **Literacy**.

As with the earlier books, used with flexibility this one is appropriate for both **Key Stages One and Two**. It provides well-planned teaching sessions with photocopiable pages, lovely illustrations and structured Circle Time and Literacy Hour learning activities. (Some schools have discontinued Literacy Hour, preferring to permeate literacy activities throughout the day. Obviously you should use the literacy sessions suggested in this book to suit your own approach.) The heroes and heroines of the stories are drawn from a diversity of ethnic groups and have a range of abilities and disabilities. Each value-theme is also used to plan for an associated **school assembly**.

Story and the curriculum

Story-telling has always been a powerful and basic human activity. In all civilisations and cultures, both the activity of story-telling and significant, individual stories have been passed down the generations. This is because, long before the printed word was available, story was the means by which people attempted to make sense of their experience of the world, to communicate that understanding and to achieve a collective wisdom through passing on accumulating knowledge and values in a memorable and accessible way.

Stories both educate and entertain. We learn from them and the learning is fun. They stimulate our imagination and teach us about ourselves, about others, about the world and about the world of values. Because learning from stories is enjoyable, children simultaneously learn to love learning. Because children feel the power of story, to make use of stories in the classroom makes sound educational sense.

Perhaps above all, the use of story is important in our understanding of ourselves and others. Stories give access to, and explore, the private realm of thought and feeling – the very realm which Circle Time aims to explore.

Circle Time

Stories can link to the curriculum in many ways. They can provide a springboard into learning for all the essential areas encapsulated in the national curriculum, including the cross-curriculum domains. In this book they are used as a springboard into some fundamental learning appropriate for Circle Time.

A majority of schools use or have used Circle Time, and there seems to be a diversity of aims and approaches to it. What, then, is Circle Time? The children form a circle or circles. The use of the circle varies from school to school. The circle may be formed spontaneously, when the teacher sees a need, or Circle Time may be timetabled – perhaps weekly or even on a daily basis. There are rules to make Circle-Time discussion work, (e.g. only speaking when holding an object such as a particular toy or a conch shell). Within the circle, games, discussion and structured activities aim to enhance children's self-esteem, self knowledge and self confidence; to develop their communication skills; to provide group participation and experience of democratic problem-solving. The circle comes to represent a secure, inclusive place. As Jenny Mosley (a great enthusiast for Circle Time) has said:

> The circle has always been a symbol of unity, healing and power. Many cultures have roots in the problem-solving, goal-achieving potential of the symbolic circle. The North American Indians used to sit in a circle with their talking object, often a feather or a pipe. Whoever was talking while holding the pipe would not have his train of thoughts interrupted by others in the circle.
>
> Jenny Mosley, *Quality Circle Time in the Classroom*, LDA, 1996; p. 70

Moreover, because Circle Time enables children to explore their own difficult emotions and experiences through their own stories, seeing these emotions and experiences reflected in these collected stories should facilitate the exploration. The children will be more willing to acknowledge their personal feelings through an identification with the child in the story.

There seems to be something democratic and safe about sitting in a circle. Circles have no top or bottom and they **contain** rather than exclude. By using this innate power of the circle as the place for discussion of important interpersonal issues in a supportive ethos, we open the way for effective emotional development of the children. To sum up, Circle Time simultaneously promotes:

- speaking, listening and discussion skills
- democratic values and skills
- a forum for democratic decisions
- a forum for problem-solving
- greater interpersonal understanding between teacher and children and between child and child.

The circle of values and relationships

The myriad curriculum and value related aims and goals of Circle Time can be expressed in terms of a widening circle of values/relationships. With the child or self at the core, the circle widens out to include "the other", "the world", and the realm of "values" itself.

Stories which embody and explore these values enable teachers to focus discussions and develop their pupils' values in an enjoyable way.

Quality Circle Time provides for a special time in the school week (or day) when children can think about their relationships and behaviour and during which they can be honest about their problems and feelings. They develop collectively agreed solutions to individual and group problems. They frequently arrive at good solutions and decisions. And some teachers already link Circle Time with Literacy Hour – using poems and stories from Literacy Hour to prompt the discussion in Circle Time.

A widening circle of values and relationships

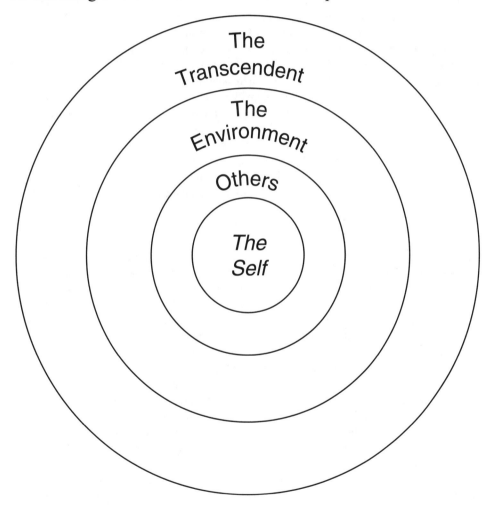

Stories drawing on each ring of the circle of values are used as a way of structuring activities to improve children's self-confidence (Ring 1), empathy and social skills (Ring 2), environmental awareness (Ring 3) and understanding of values (Ring 4). In so doing, these Circle activities provide the opportunity for children to practise the skills of listening, expressing their own feeling and views and cooperating with others. Moreover, some of the suggested activities enable children to name and solve personal, classroom and school problems and dilemmas.

Literacy (Hour)

While all educators acknowledge the huge instrumental and intrinsic value of becoming literate, how children best learn to speak, read and write is complex, fascinating and hotly debated. What is generally agreed is that children learn best when motivated, and that "Oracy" (speaking and listening) is part of "literacy". Children are interested in hearing and telling stories. These stories provide a ready springboard for discussion. Discussion of the stories must include open, thought-provoking (rather than merely closed, factual) questions that stimulate thinking and reveal a variety of points of view.

In any case, story is central to literature. We want children to explore the characteristics of language in story telling. Thus particular child-friendly stories (such as those in this collection) can provide a literacy resource for increasing the children's understanding of story and enable them to develop a meta-language with which to discuss stories. They can discuss, with increasing fluency and understanding, plot, theme, narrative structure, vocabulary, sentence structure, character and dialogue.

The children will first notice the story's character and what happens to them (plot), and can be led from this to notice the theme and aspects of style and narrative convention.

For all these reasons, "stories and literacy" are as inherently compatible as "motivation and learning" or "meaning and communication" or "language and world".

Circle Time and Literacy (Hour) links

Why bring Circle Time and Literacy (Hour) together in this one book? The emphasis on **communication** in both is the main reason. This shared emphasis encourages a natural link between Circle Time and literacy, the most important area of the curriculum. Indeed, teachers already link literacy and Circle Time, using games and stories from Literacy Hour to prompt discussion in Circle Time, for example. This book encourages Circle Time to feed into literacy too – a mutual, ongoing interaction.

Story, and its inherent emphasis on values and emotions, resonates, as we have seen, with the personal, social and emotional goals of Circle Time; story is also an important ingredient for Literacy Hour. Story is both at the heart of literature and a powerful tool for the development of literacy. Thus to use story in the service of both Circle Time and Literacy Hour is appropriate for each, and, brought together, allows for cross fertilisation. It also enables children to see the same theme in different contexts. The self-expression explored in "Let My Lion Out" emerges, in Circle Time, as the way in which outward behaviour expresses our inner world of feelings and can take positive and negative forms – allowing children to acknowledge and explore their own negative feelings. In Literacy Hour, self-expression is seen to motivate the creation of poems, plays, stories. I also hope that the multifaceted nature of the stories will enhance the potential for each teacher's own creative linking of Circle Time and Literacy sessions.

How to use the book

Ten new stories are grouped so as to focus on each ring of the circle of values. Two focus on the self, four on "others", two on the world/environment and two on the realm of values. The aspects covered are as follows:

The Self: Self value
1 Self-esteem
2 Self-expression

The "Other": Valuing others
3 Empathy
4 Compassion/Care
5 Family and Friendship relationships
6 Cooperation

The World: Valuing the environment
7 Protecting the environment
8 Appreciation of the natural world

The Realm of Values: Valuing the transcendent
9 Circle Time values: Democracy
10 The value of "Value": Appreciation of the circle of values

These story themes are interpreted first for Circle Time and then for Literacy Hour.

Theme	Circle Time	Literacy Hour
1 Self-esteem	Appreciation of one's own and others' value and strengths	Listening and Speaking ("Oracy") with confidence
2 Self-expression	Expressing one's feelings/emotions	Creative self-expression (using words)
3 Empathy	Understanding others	Understanding character in story
4 Compassion	Kindness to others	Caring about the character
5 Relationship	Interpersonal relationships	Working in pairs/Dialogue
6 Cooperation	Cooperating with the Circle Time group	Working in groups
7 Protecting the environment	Protecting the classroom environment	Protecting the wider environment – and uses of literacy to do so
8 Appreciation of the natural world	Appreciating/enhancing our classroom and world	Using wonder in stories. The wonder of story
9 Democracy	Circle Time democracy	Literacy for democracy
10 Value	Valuing skills and people	The intrinsic value of literature

Flexibility

Each of these ten stories is the focus for two teaching sessions: i.e. one Circle Time and one Literacy Hour. The twenty sessions should be used to suit your teaching schedule. For example, you could use two sessions per week for ten weeks. Each session provides a story, some points for discussion, and follow-up associated educational activities. Though approximate times are suggested for these activities, obviously you should set a pace which suits you and your class.

The intention is to save you time by providing good "learning" material for classroom work and for the school assembly, but you can be flexible in how you use this material. For instance, you may prefer a different sequence – perhaps because some of the later stories link with work you are currently doing and therefore could be used first.

The sessions

- Having introduced the theme of the story you can tell *or* read it.
- The children could sit in a circle for the story and discussion time.
- Deal with "difficult" vocabulary in your usual way. This often means explaining words as you come to them in the story.
- You may or may not want to ask the *closed* (comprehension-type) questions to check understanding. You may want to ask some of them as you read, or only after you have finished reading, or not at all.
- You can select or add to the more *open* "points for discussion" – according to those aspects of the theme most relevant to your curriculum.
- You can select or add to the suggested activities. Some activities could be used in follow-up lessons.
- You may wish to use the classroom activity partly as preparation for the relevant assembly. Suggestions are given.
- For the assembly, suggested poems and songs are given, taken from commonly used texts. However, should you have different poetry and songbooks in your school, you will find that it is not difficult to find poems and songs which are relevant to the themes. One of the activities for each session encourages the children themselves to make this selection – an educative task!
- You can involve the children as active participants in the assembly to different degrees, commensurate with the custom in your school.
- You can link the themes with each other and with other on-going projects. For example, themes three, four, five and six could be part of a PSE project. Stories six and twelve feature a hearing-impaired girl and an emotionally and behaviourally disturbed boy, respectively. Stories three, four and five feature an Asian fairy, an African-Caribbean family and an Asian boy, respectively. All these stories thus contribute to an inclusive, multicultural education. The story and theme of five will be useful in Development Education, of four in Family Learning projects and of seven in Environment Education. Finally, story nine contributes to Citizenship Education, and eight and ten to Religious Education.

Age levels

The material is intended for use at Key Stages One and Two. Since this includes a relatively wide age range (4–11 years), use the material at the developmental level appropriate for your children. A class of younger children may "tell" rather than "write" their own stories and learn to recognise key words. Older children, on the other hand, will be able to write their own associated stories and poems and may even take a turn in reading part of the theme story in the classroom or assembly.

Precious time

The book is intended to be a useful and *time-saving* resource for classroom and assembly. I am sure that, like all learning/teaching resources, it will be used in a whole variety of different ways. Some teachers may reach for the book as the basis for a morning's work on those (rare but inevitable!) occasions when they have simply not had time to prepare material of their own. Other teachers may take each story/activity as the starting point for an extended project on the highlighted theme. Or it may be their turn to prepare an assembly. Some schools may wish to use the resource in a whole-school approach to emotional educational and/or literacy. They may encourage parents to use the book to work with their child. The book could provide bedtime or rainy-day stories with the bonus of discussion points and associated educational activities. In particular, it should enrich Circle Time and Literacy work. In whatever way you choose to use it, I hope that you and the children will enjoy the theme-stories and the activities, and that these will genuinely promote the development of those worthwhile values, skills and attitudes which are part of a balanced education.

Chapter 1

A Cool Call

Circle Time One

Teacher's Notes

Theme One:	The value of **Self-confidence**
Circle Time Value:	The development of self-confidence is a Circle Time aim. The self is at the centre of our Circle of Values. The development of self-confidence is part of **Personal Education.**

> **Circle Time provides a forum in which each child can be listened to, understood and valued. The development of self-confidence is important for a child's learning, well-being and success. It requires the development of a positive self-image, which is encouraged by progress and by praise and achievement.**

Circle Time Plan

This five-part lesson plan is only a guide. Teachers are likely to add to or amend the learning activities which are suggested and may sometimes wish to substitute their own. For any part of the session they may wish to allow more or less time than that suggested.

1 Introduce the theme   *3–6 minutes*

What is **self-confidence**, and how can we help each other to be more confident in Circle Time?

2 Vocabulary   *3–6 minutes*

The teacher ensures that the children understand the words given.

3 The story   *6 minutes*

The teacher shows the illustration and reads the story.

4 Talking about the story   *10–20 minutes*

The teacher uses some of the questions and discussion points given, stimulating the children to talk about the story/theme.

5 The Circle Time learning activity   *10–20 minutes*

These activities encourage listening skills, praise and appreciation, and dealing with insults. Some suggested activities could be used in follow-up lessons.

Total time	*30–60 minutes (approx.)*

1 INTRODUCE THE THEME

Key points

- Each one of us is a valuable human being with our own ideas, points of view and interests. We are all good at some things and not so good at others.

- In Circle Time we all learn to speak out and we must all be good at listening too.

- What is self-confidence? (Contrast this with shyness but also with vanity.) What can we do to help someone who is shy to speak out?

2 VOCABULARY

Use your usual methods for introducing new words.

The difficult words in the story are:

sneaking	-	*passing something secretly*
whirring	-	*buzzing/whizzing sound*
anxiously	-	*worriedly*
hunched	-	*shoulders bent over*
dopey	-	*slow thinking; stupid*
blurted	-	*spoke suddenly – without thinking first*
muttered	-	*spoke unclearly with mouth nearly closed*
sympathy	-	*feeling for another in pain*
scrabbled	-	*scraped at with paws (hands)*
freshly	-	*recently; not new*
pounced	-	*jumped on; sprang upon suddenly*
training	-	*teaching skills; instructing*

3 THE STORY:

A Cool Call

A Cool Call

Dylan was sneaking a piece of roast beef to Tippy, his dog, when he heard a whirring noise like a camera.

"Look Dylan," Robert said, "I've taken your photo."

Dylan took Robert's phone. On the small screen he could see a picture of himself.

"Good, huh?" said Dad.

Dylan nodded. He reached across the table to hand back the phone. It slipped from his fingers and plopped into a white jug where it disappeared beneath hot gravy.

"You clumsy dope!" Robert yelled.

Dylan cringed and Tippy growled at Robert, who fished the phone out of the gravy. He wiped it with kitchen paper and tested it. Dylan watched anxiously.

"It's OK," Robert said.

"Come on, Rob," said Dad, "let's finish gardening."

It was quiet after they'd gone. Dylan hunched at the table, lost in thought. He was remembering the time he got all his sums wrong again and the teacher had been cross.

"He can't help it, Sir," Adam had said. "Old Dopey Dylan."

"Be quiet, Adam," said the teacher, but the nickname had stuck.

"Cheer up, Dylan." His Mum's voice brought him back to the present. She was smiling at him, though her eyes looked troubled.

"You can have a camera phone, too," she said. "For your birthday."

Dylan bent and stroked Tippy. She had been his best birthday present ever. Tippy thumped her tail on the floor.

"Robert didn't mean to shout, love," said Mum.

"That's what they call me at school," Dylan blurted out. He hadn't really meant to tell her.

"Call you what?" she said.

"Dopey Dylan," he muttered, and he felt himself go red.

"Well, you're not!" Mum said. She sounded angry, but not with him.

"I'm no good at anything though," said Dylan. "Not like Robert."

Tippy nudged his leg in sympathy and Mum gave him a hug. Before she could say anything, Dad stuck his head round the door.

"Hey, you two. Come and help. Rob's lost his phone."

All four members of the family began to search around the garden. Robert looked very upset. Dylan longed to be the one to find the phone for his brother. Suddenly, something he had seen on telly flashed in his mind.

"Ring Rob's number, Dad," he said. "On your mobile."

Dad stared at Dylan and a big grin spread across his face.

"Brilliant idea son. Why didn't I think of that?"

Dad dialed and they all listened.

Dylan heard it first. The ringing was under the ground, over by the rose bushes.

"Fetch," he said to Tippy, pointing at the bushes. Tippy ran over and scrabbled at the freshly dug earth, scattering it behind her. She pounced on something, ran to Dylan and dropped it at his feet.

Dylan picked it up, wiped it clean on his jeans and walked over to Robert.

"Your phone, bro'," he said, holding it out.

"Thank you, Dylan," said Robert. "That was cool."

Dylan was pleased. He bent and patted Tippy, hiding his big smile.

"Good dog," he said, stroking her. Tippy wagged her tail. She was grinning too.

Later, when Mum came up to say goodnight, she sat down on Dylan's bed.

"Making the phone ring was a brilliant idea, Dylan," she said. "Even Dad and Robert didn't think of that."

"Yeah," Dylan said, smiling. "It was cool."

"And," said Mum, "Tippy knew exactly what you wanted her to do. That's because you've trained her so well. That's something you're good at, you know, very good."

"What?" said Dylan.

"Training dogs, of course."

At that moment the door was pushed open and in came Tippy. She jumped up on the bed. Usually Mum sent her downstairs but this time she said, "OK. She can stay. Sleep well, Dylan."

Mum clicked off the light and went downstairs. Tippy curled up beside Dylan. He stroked her for a long time, feeling happy. Training dogs was a great thing to be good at, and perhaps Mum would let Tippy sleep on his bed every night from now on.

4 TALKING ABOUT THE STORY

Did the children understand?

- Why did Robert call Dylan a "clumsy dope"?

- Why was Dylan very upset about this?

- What was Dylan's good idea?

- How did Tippy help?

- What was Dylan good at?

Points for discussion

- Discuss the importance of names and the cruelty of name-calling, which is a form of bullying. What should you do about name-calling? Would anyone like to apologise for using a bad name? (The child should apologise to the other child without using the bad name, e.g. "I'm sorry for what I said John". Or, "I'm sorry I called you a bad name, John". The apology should only be made if it is sincere. This means that the name-caller will not do this name-calling again.)

- What should we call people in Circle Time? Why is this important?

- What are we all good at? Go round the circle so that each child can say something that they are good at and something another child is good at. The teacher could go round and say something that each child is good at, or that those not yet mentioned are good at.

5 THE CIRCLE TIME LEARNING ACTIVITY

1   Warm-up game

Chinese whispers: Listening skills

The teacher whispers a sentence to the child on his/her left. The child whispers to the next child, and so on up to the child on the teacher's right. This child and the teacher compare sentences. Has it come back correctly? If not, the teacher can send round a second sentence. Choose sentences which reinforce the theme. E.g. Everyone here is good at something.

2   Circle contribution

Praise in pairs: One good thing

Each child forms a pair with a neighbouring child in the circle. They spend five minutes each asking questions to find out more about the other child – especially things like: What are you good at? What "good turns" have you done this week? How have you helped someone at home/at school recently? What have you done or made that you are pleased about?

After five minutes of this research, the teacher goes round the circle. Each child says one good thing they have learned about their partner.

3   Circle discussion

Dealing with insults

Talk about how Dylan felt about being called a bad name. Talk about how we can deal with insults. E.g. ignore the insult as though you don't care; make a joke in response; just smile and carry on with what you are doing; walk away.

In pairs, the children should think of ways of dealing with an insult and pick one each to share with the class. Go round the circle sharing these and let this activity lead into a group discussion.

4   Circle group work

A positive portrait (resources needed: paint or crayons or pencils)

The children should each do a portrait of the child whose name comes after their name in the register. This can be done in pencil, crayons or paint, but it should be a very **positive** portrait.

Each child takes a turn to show their portrait and to say what they like about the child portrayed. The other children may then say what they like about the portrait.

A Cool Call

Literacy Hour One

Teacher's Notes

Theme One: The value of **Communication**

Literacy Skills: Self-confidence helps children to communicate.

> **Literacy Hour provides a regular time in which children can practise their speaking, reading and writing – including the achievement of self-confidence in the oral skills of conversation, debate and reading aloud.**

Literacy Hour Plan

This five-part lesson plan is only a guide. Teachers are likely to add to or amend the learning activities which are suggested and may sometimes wish to substitute their own. For any part of the session they may wish to allow more or less time than that suggested.

1 Introduce the theme *3–6 minutes*

How can we become more self-confident in conversation? Debate? Reading aloud?

2 Vocabulary *3–6 minutes*

Can the children produce synonyms, antonyms and sentences for the difficult words (which were covered in the Circle Time session)?

3 The story *6 minutes*

This could be told or read by the children.

4 Talking about the story *10–20 minutes*

The teacher uses some of the questions and discussion points given, stimulating the children to talk about the story as a narrative. This helps the children to develop a (literary) meta-language.

5 The Literacy Time learning activity *10–20 minutes*

Some of the suggested "literacy" activities encourage group work as a positive enhancement of the Circle Time skills and values. Some of the activities could be used in follow-up lessons.

| **Total time** | *30–60 minutes (approx.)* |

1 INTRODUCE THE THEME

Key points

- Why is interactive oral communication important in daily life, for example:

  (i)   In conversation?

  (ii) In phone messages?

  (iii) In debate?

- How can we become more confident in using these skills (e.g. practice, learning from others, etc.)?

2 VOCABULARY

Can you think of a word(s) that means the same as/the opposite to each of these? For each of the words, make up a sentence containing that word.

sneaking	whirring
anxious	blurted
hunched	muttered
dopey	sympathy
fresh	scrabbled
pounced	training

3   THE STORY:

With younger children – ask them to use their own words to tell the story (*Cool Call*) which they listened to in Circle Time. With older children, go round the class having the children (re-) read the story out loud. Alternatively, give the children time to (re-) read the story to themselves.

A Cool Call

4   TALKING ABOUT THE STORY

Did the children understand?

- Why did Tippy growl at Robert?

- Why was Dylan anxious when Robert tested his phone?

- Why do you think that Dylan's Mum let Tippy stay on Dylan's bed?

Points for discussion

- What is a sub-text in a story? (Explain that a sub-text is what we are told indirectly.) We work it out from what we are told directly. Give examples of sub-text, e.g.:

  Teacher: "This is quite good, Ann." (sub-text: "I know you can do better.")
  Get the children to give examples.

- What is the sub-text in these lines?
  "Cheer up, Dylan." His Mum's voice brought him back to the present. She was smiling at him, though her eyes looked troubled.
  and
  "That's what they call me at school," Dylan blurted out. He hadn't really meant to tell her. "Call you what?" she said.
  "Dopey Dylan," he muttered, and he felt himself go red.

- What, for you, is the message of this story? (Examples: We are all good at something. Name calling hurts. Mums can be brilliant.) The children should understand that there is not just one correct answer.

5   THE LEARNING ACTIVITY

1   **Songs and Poems** (resources needed: poetry or song anthologies)

In pairs or small groups, find a poem or song which connects with the story. (It could be about name-calling, pets, telephones, skills – i.e. things I can do.) Ask some of the children to read out their chosen poem or song.

2   **Story discussion**

Clear information

Discuss why it is more difficult to communicate **clearly** on the telephone. (There are no visual clues on the phone, e.g. facial expression; arm movements.)
   In pairs the children should practise giving and receiving clear information. For example:

- There is a fire in the house. Dial 999. What details must you remember to give? Fire/Address/Number of people in house.

- You are ill and must order the family groceries over the phone. What details must you give? Address/Correct identification of goods, e.g. large box of cornflakes (which brand?).

3   Individual activity

Write a description

Write a description, using only positive words, of another child in the class. The teacher could give each child a slip with the name of the child to be described. This will ensure every child is included.

N.B. These descriptions could be used in the next Circle Time, as children take it in turns to read their description while the class must "guess who".

4   Group activity

(i) **Dialogue** (resources needed: pens and paper)
     In pairs the children should write a dialogue between Dylan and Robert. Dylan has his own mobile phone now. Robert is away from home on a school week-end residential. They are on their mobiles to each other, to plan a surprise for Mum's birthday. Her birthday is on the day after Robert gets back.

(ii) **Write a play** (resources needed: pens and paper)
     The children are going to turn the story, Cool Call, into a play. There are four scenes.

Scene One	In the kitchen. (Dylan, Robert, Mum, Dad, Tippy) The action up to Dad and Robert going into the garden.
Scene Two	In the kitchen. (Dylan, Mum, Tippy, Dad, possibly Adam and Teacher) Dylan tells Mum about his mean nickname, "Dopey Dylan". The children will need to think about how to tell us about Adam. Does Dylan tell Mum or do we "see" his flashback at the front of stage. Dad pops his head in to call for help in finding Robert's phone.
Scene Three	In the garden. (Dad, Mum, Dylan, Robert, Tippy) The finding of the phone.
Scene Four	In Dylan's bedroom. (Mum, Dylan, Tippy) Mum reminds Dylan he is good at training dogs, and Tippy gets to sleep on his bed.

Divide the class into four (or eight) groups. Each group writes an allocated scene and brings the play together (in a play reading) at the end. If you have eight smaller groups, one of the two versions of each scene can be voted for and the resulting play acted out.
   (Younger children could draw their scene, in a small group, and the class would come together to pin these up in the correct sequence.)

A Cool Call

Assembly

Theme: Respect for Each Other

Introduction

The assembly leader introduces the theme and talks about why we should respect each other. We are all human beings with feelings and our own ideas. We are all good at some things and not at others. Give examples of showing respect: listening well to others; giving praise whenever it is deserved; not calling names.

Story

Assembly leader

Our story today is about Dylan, a boy who thought there was nothing he was good at but who found out that there was. Dylan's Mum is good at seeing what other people can do. She shows respect for all her family.

The assembly leader or a child reads the story – *Cool Call*.

Poem or Song

You can choose a poem or a song, or both. Alternatively, you can have a child (or children) read the poems they chose or wrote in class and have one of the songs that were chosen. Select poems and songs which are relevant to the theme or which echo the story in some way.

Examples

Poem:

The Name Game
Page 88 in *Smile, Please!* by Tony Bradman, published by Puffin Books, 1989.

Song:

I Can Climb
No. 17 in *Every Colour Under the Sun*, published by Ward Lock Educational Co. Ltd, 1983.

Quiet reflection or prayer

For a universal, humanistic or multi-faith assembly:

Quiet reflection

The assembly leader says:
"Think for a moment about how we feel when someone praises us for something well done. (Pause) Think of how we feel if someone calls us a bad name or says something mean. (Pause) Let us think for a moment about what we are good at. (Pause) Think for a moment

about what our teacher, our friend, the people in our family are good at. (Pause) Let us remember to praise when we can and not to use bad names to anyone at all."

Or for Christian schools:

Prayer

Let us pray.

Dear Heavenly Father,
Who made each one of us and who created our world, help us to respect ourselves and each other and help us to respect the plants and flowers and creatures of your creation.

Amen.

Chapter 2

Let My Lion Out

Circle Time Two

Teacher's Notes

Theme Two: The value of **Self-expression**

Circle Time Value: Learning to express our feelings is part of our
emotional education.

> Circle Time provides a forum in which we can learn to understand our
> emotions. As we learn more about who we are, simultaneously we begin to
> develop our understanding of other people (the next ring in our circle of
> values). In addition, creative self-expression opens the door to aesthetic
> values and will be explored in the linked literacy hour.

Circle Time Plan

This five-part lesson plan is only a guide. Teachers are likely to add to or amend the learning activities which are suggested and may sometimes wish to substitute their own. For any
part of the session they may wish to allow more or less time than that suggested.

1 Introduce the theme   *3–6 minutes*

What is **self-expression**? The teacher can talk about positive and
negative ways of expressing our feelings. She can give examples
and encourage examples from the children.

2 Vocabulary   *3–6 minutes*

The teacher ensures that the children understand the words given.

3 The story   *6 minutes*

The teacher shows the illustration and reads the story.

4 Talking about the story   *10–20 minutes*

The teacher uses some of the questions and discussion points given,
stimulating the children to talk about the story/theme.

5 The Circle Time learning activity   *10–20 minutes*

The activities will encourage children to use Circle Time to explore
and understand their own emotions and to gain insight into, and
sympathy for, the feelings of others. Some suggested activities could
be used in follow-up lessons.

| **Total time** | *30–60 minutes (approx.)* |

1 INTRODUCE THE THEME

Key points

- There are two related senses of self-expression.
  1   We learn to recognise, understand and express our deep feelings in positive ways. This is linked to a development in self-knowledge.
  2   We learn to be creative; we express **ourselves** because we make something no one else would make in exactly the same way.

- In learning more about our own emotions we also learn to understand more about other people's feelings too.

2 VOCABULARY

Use your usual methods for introducing new words.

The difficult words in the story are:

snatched	–	*grabbed*
wicker	–	*woven cane*
frustration	–	*disappointment; bafflement; being thwarted*
lurched	–	*staggered*
swaggered	–	*boastful walk; strutted*
furious	–	*very angry*
swelled	–	*expand (like wave of sea)*
calm	–	*still, quiet, peaceful*
match	–	*fit; go together*
charging	–	*attacking onrush*
roaring	–	*loud, deep, hoarse sound, as of a lion*
baited	–	*enticed with food – to annoy and trap*
dangerous	–	*risky*
dealt with	–	*sorted out*

3 THE STORY:

Let My Lion Out

Let My Lion Out

Alison snatched Edward's last piece of toast. He was furious, but before he could argue Mum plonked a wicker basket in the middle of the table.

"Look," she said. "I've won a raffle."

She began to unpack the goods: wine, cheese and jars of jam. There was also a bar of chocolate and a red notebook.

"Tell you what, kids," she said. "You can have the notebook and the chocolate. One each."

"Ta Mum," said Alison, grabbing the chocolate and scooting off.

"That's not fair," Edward shouted. "I wanted the chocolate. We should have half each."

"Have the notebook instead," said Mum.

"Who wants a lousy notebook?" Edward said, and he swore under his breath.

"Language," Mum hit the table with the flat of her hand. "I won't tell you again."

Edward felt his whole body clench with frustration. His horrible sister had snatched all the chocolate, and he was the one getting told off!

Angry and fed up, Edward trudged to school. He had almost reached the school gates when Brigs Barker pushed him off the pavement! His heart lurched as a car coming out of school almost hit him. The driver gave a long, angry hoot. Brigs swaggered on, leaving Edward feeling more furious than ever. Brigs, who was bigger, often picked on Edward, which wasn't fair. But this had been dangerous! Things often made Edward angry these days and he hated the hot feelings that swelled in his head.

Once inside school Edward tried to calm down for his first lesson.

"Today, we're going to write a poem", said Mrs Makibi, "about how we feel."

Edward frowned. *What a lousy idea*, he thought.

"For example," said the teacher, "how do you feel, Edward, right now?"

"Pretty mad," he said, which made everyone laugh.

"Mad as a hatter, or mad as a bear with a sore head?" asked the teacher.

"A bear with a sore head," Edward said.

"Good. Anger will give you plenty to write about."

Now Edward even felt angry with his nice teacher. How could he write about Alison and toast, or Brigs?

"We're all going to think of animals who match our feelings. Take anger, which Edward is feeling. What animal would match?"

"A charging bull," said Nazreen. In spite of himself, Edward saw that she was right. A charging bull did look just like he felt.

"Good," said the teacher.

She made the children write down one feeling and three animals to go with it. Edward wrote **Anger** and "a bear with a sore head" and "a charging bull". That was easy because Mrs Makibi and Nazreen had given him the ideas. What about his third animal, though? He thought about the film he'd seen at the weekend. The roaring lion at the beginning seemed angry. He wrote "roaring lion" on his page.

"Your poems needn't rhyme," Mrs Makibi said. "In fact it's probably better if they don't."

Edward, in his cross mood, immediately decided that his would rhyme if he could manage it and, for the first time ever, he wrote a poem quite easily. He even liked it. He made some small changes and liked it more. By the time he had finished, his anger had completely vanished.

Mrs Makibi liked Edward's poem. She read it to the class.

Not Fair

Like a charging bull
Or like a baited bear
I'm red in my head
Because it's not fair.
I feel a roaring rage
Like a lion in a cage
I want to stamp and shout
And let my lion out.

Mrs Makibi said it was good enough to go on the "best work" wall, and she pinned it up. Edward was pleased.

"Some people take their anger out on others," said Mrs Makibi. "That's called bullying. I saw a dangerous bit of bullying this morning. It's being dealt with." She smiled at Edward. Somehow he knew she meant Brigs and he felt even more pleased.

The Story

At tea-time Edward told Mum about the poem. She was pleased too. He wrote it in the red notebook and even Alison said it was good. Edward had found a way to cool down his anger by writing his feelings into a poem. The red notebook would be useful after all.

4 TALKING ABOUT THE STORY

Did the children understand?

- What two actions did Edward think unfair?

- How did Edward nearly have a dangerous accident?

- What three animals did Edward use in his poem?

- Why did Edward want to make his poem rhyme?

- In the end, for what purpose did Edward decide to use his new red notebook?

Points for discussion

- How many of you have felt angry? What about? What did it feel like? What did you do?

- How can we use Circle Time to deal with things that have made us angry in school?

- Why might writing a poem help us to cool off our anger?

- How can we use Circle Time to deal with bullying?

5 THE CIRCLE TIME LEARNING ACTIVITY

1   Warm-up game

Colour and music

The teacher should have charts with a large expanse of such colours as red, blue, green, grey, yellow. As you show each colour, go round the circle and ask the children to say what feeling that colour makes them think of. Any child who wishes can say why. E.g. yellow makes me think of "happy" because it is bright and cheerful. The teacher could also play different types of taped music and ask the same question.

2   Circle contribution

Happy/Sad (resources needed: large sheets of white paper, coloured pens)

Discuss a range of emotions with the children. What emotions can they think of? Being frightened, angry, surprised, disappointed, worried, sorry (apologetic and sympathy) etc., **and** happy and sad.

Have the children ever felt happy? What made them feel happy?

Go round the circle asking the children to complete the sentence: "I feel happy when…"

Have the children ever felt sad? What makes them feel sad?

Go round the circle asking the children to complete the sentence: "I feel sad when…"

How can we cheer people up? Link this with kindness. Kind people help others to feel happier and they feel happier themselves.

How can we treat each other to make a happy classroom?

Using bright, happy colours, write down the children's suggestions to form a poster for the wall. (In a subsequent Art session the children could draw small colourful pictures to illustrate the suggestions on the poster as illustrative decoration.)

In a subsequent Circle Time a poster could be made for a happy **playground**.

The teacher could ask if anyone feels unhappy about anything in the playground that they would like help with.

3   Circle discussion

That's not fair

Edward felt angry when Alison and Brigs were unfair. Discuss with the children why unfair behaviour makes us angry. Go round the circle asking the children to give an example of something that wasn't fair.

How can we learn to be fair? (E.g. Sharing. Voting. Doing as you would be done by.) Go round the circle asking the children to given an example of being fair (e.g. to their friend, or even to someone they don't like!).

4   Circle group work

Dealing with bullying

Discuss the forms that this kind of bad behaviour can take, eliciting suggestions from the children: name-calling (like in *Cool Call*), shoving and picking on someone (like in *Let My Lion Out*), hitting, throwing something at someone, saying nasty things, leaving someone out, not talking to someone, etc.

Go round the circle asking children to complete the sentence: "When I am bullied I feel…"

Discuss how we can deal with bullying. Again encourage suggestions. Walk away. Ignore. Discuss with a sympathetic adult (teacher or relative, etc.).

Write suggestions on an **Anti-Bullying Advice Chart** for the wall.

Finally, you could give the children the address and telephone number of some advice lines. For example:

Kidscape
152 Buckingham Palace Road
London
SW1W 9TR
Tel: 020 7730 3300
Mon–Fri 10.00 am to 4.00 pm

Kidscape is a helpline for parents of bullied or bullying children. Send an SAE for three free booklets about bullying.

Free Helplines (won't show up on the telephone bill):
Child Line: 0800 1111
Samaritans: 0345 909090

Let My Lion Out

Literacy Hour Two

Teacher's Notes

Theme Two: The value of creative **self-expression**

Literacy Skills: Creative self-expression, using the medium of language – in poetry, story, song, etc. This is an important element of aesthetic education.

> **Literacy Hour provides a regular time in which children can engage with words to make/create a poem or a story, etc.**

Literacy Hour Plan

This five-part lesson plan is only a guide. Teachers are likely to add to or amend the learning activities which are suggested and may sometimes wish to substitute their own. For any part of the session they may wish to allow more or less time than that suggested.

1 Introduce the theme   *3–6 minutes*

We can express our feelings and ideas in words. Using words we can create a poem or a story as well as we possibly can.

2 Vocabulary   *3–6 minutes*

Can the children produce synonyms, antonyms and sentences for the difficult words (which were covered in the Circle Time session)?

3 The story   *6 minutes*

This could be told or read by the children.

4 Talking about the story   *10–20 minutes*

The teacher uses some of the questions and discussion points given, stimulating the children to talk about the story as a narrative. This helps the children to develop a (literary) meta-language.

5 The Literacy Time learning activity   *10–20 minutes*

Some of the suggested "literacy" activities encourage group work as a positive enhancement of the Circle Time skills and values. Some of the activities could be used in follow-up lessons.

Total time | *30–60 minutes (approx.)*

1 INTRODUCE THE THEME

Key points

- There are two aspects to being creative with words (writing a play, a poem or a story). First we make something unique because no one else would write exactly the same. Second, we write it as well as we can so that others will want to read it. It must be clear and interesting.

- Give examples of using language/words as well as we can. (E.g. using our imagination for new ideas to express, choosing interesting words, using vivid words, creating new phrases and similes, etc.).

2 VOCABULARY

Can you think of a word(s) that means the same as/the opposite to each of these? For each of the words, make up a sentence containing that word.

snatched	whicker
lurched	frustration
furious	swaggered
swelled	calm
match	changing
baited	roaring
dangerous	dealt with

3 THE STORY:

With younger children – ask them to use their own words to tell the story (*Let My Lion Out*) which they listened to in Circle Time. With older children, go round the class having the children (re-) read the story out loud. Alternatively, give the children time to (re-) read the story to themselves.

Let My Lion Out

4 TALKING ABOUT THE STORY

Did the children understand?

- Why did Edward think Alison had been unfair?

- What different things might someone mean if they say someone is "mad"? (Ill/ disturbed/angry.) Discuss how we use negative language about mental illness – e.g. mad, loony, crazy – and that this is unfair and mean, a kind of name-calling.

- What two different ways does the image of "a charging bull" match Edward's anger? (A charging bull looks angry. His anger feels like there is a charging bull inside him.)

- How does Edward know Mrs Makibi had dealt with Brigs?

Points for discussion

- Do you think Mrs Makibi was a good teacher? (The children should give reasons based on the story.)

- What does Edward mean by "And let my lion out"?

- Why do you think the story writer made the notebook red?

- If a poem doesn't rhyme, what would make it a poem?

- What, for you, is the message of this story? (E.g. It is good to use negative feelings to create poems. It is good to overcome negative emotions by expressing them in a poem. Unfair behaviour makes people angry, etc. It is mean, unfair and even dangerous to bully someone.) The children should understand that there is not just one correct answer.

5 THE LEARNING ACTIVITY

1 **Songs and Poems** (resources needed: poetry or song anthologies)

In pairs or small groups, find a poem or song which connects with the story. (It could be about anger, emotion, poetry, creativity, unfairness, bullying.) Ask some of the children to read out their chosen poem or song.

2 **Poem discussion**

Write a poem

The children can write their own poems about their feelings. They can choose a feeling they have experienced and find an animal and/or a colour and/or weather which matches it, and use these ideas to write their own poem. These can be read out loud to the class and discussed. Which matches work? Which poems did they like? Why?

3   Individual activity

Write a letter

The children should be given a photocopy of the letter on page 35 and pretend it is a letter from a pen-friend. They should reply to the letter, giving advice. They can use ideas from the Anti-Bullying Advice Chart constructed in Circle Time.

4   Group activity

- Read out (or ask the children to read) the letters which give good and useful advice. Encourage the children to discuss these. You could write up a list of the ideas which the children think would work best.

NB. Does your school use "squabble busters" (children who are trained to deal with playground issues such as friends falling-out, fighting, etc.)? If not, you might want to consider this approach.

Dear Pen-Friend,

Thanks for your last letter. I enjoyed all your news and I'm glad you are well. I had a good holiday but, now we're back at school, all I can think about is the horrid bullying that is going on. Several kids get bullied here, including me. Some of the kids call me four-eyes and I don't like it. Also, sometimes two bigger boys push me about a bit in the playground. It's not fair but I'm not sure what to do. I don't want to tell tales but it could get worse. Any ideas?

Best wishes,

Jack

Let My Lion Out
Assembly

Theme: Positive Self-Expression

Introduction

The assembly leader introduces the theme and talks about how we should express ourselves in positive ways – using our good emotions to be expressed in kind actions, and controlling our negative feelings. Expressing these in creative self-expression is better than expressing them in bad behaviour.

Story

Assembly leader:

Our story today is about Edward, a boy who was angry. We can understand why unfairness and bullying made Edward angry, but Edward succeeded in expressing his anger in a poem which everyone liked.

The assembly leader or a child reads the story – *Let My Lion Out.*

Poem or Song

You can choose a poem or a song, or both. Alternatively, you can have a child (or children) read the poems they chose or wrote in class and have one of the songs that were chosen; or Edward's poem could be read, or some of the poems written by the children in Literacy Hour. Select poems and songs which are relevant to the theme or which echo the story in some way.

Examples

Poem:

The Quarrel
Page 26 in *A First Poetry Book*, published by Oxford University Press, 1991.

Song:

Getting Angry
No. 46 in *Every Colour Under The Sun*, published by Ward Lock Educational Co. Ltd., 1983.

Quiet reflection or prayer

For a universal, humanistic or multi-faith assembly:

Quiet reflection

The assembly leader says:

"Think of how you feel if someone is angry with you. (Pause) Or is kind to you. (Pause) Positive emotions help us to feel happy and to make other people feel happy. Let us think of ways we can chill out our negative emotions. (Pause) Let us think of how we can be both kind and fair to our friends, classmates and family. (Pause)"

Or for Christian schools:

Prayer

Let us pray.

Almighty God,
Help us to feel loving and happy and to keep our actions kind and fair. Give us the strength to express our negative feelings in positive ways. Thank you for the wonderful poems and songs and stories which people have made for us to enjoy.

Amen.

Chapter 3

The Magic Bead

Circle Time Three

Teacher's Notes

Theme Three: The value of **Empathy**

Circle Time Value: We move out from valuing the self to valuing others. The development of empathy (sympathetic understanding) is a major step forward in a child's social/moral education.

Circle Time provides a forum in which each child should be listened to with empathy. The development of empathy is important for a child's social interactions and relationships and is encouraged by recognition that others feel as we do in similar situations.

Circle Time Plan

This five-part lesson plan is only a guide. Teachers are likely to add to or amend the learning activities which are suggested and may sometimes wish to substitute their own. For any part of the session they may wish to allow more or less time than that suggested.

1 Introduce the theme   *3–6 minutes*

What is **empathy**? (understanding with sympathy) Why is empathy important in Circle Time? (link with trust) How can we show empathy in Circle Time?

2 Vocabulary   *3–6 minutes*

The teacher ensures that the children understand the words given.

3 The story   *6 minutes*

The teacher shows the illustration and reads the story.

4 Talking about the story   *10–20 minutes*

The teacher uses some of the questions and discussion points given, stimulating the children to talk about the story/theme.

5 The Circle Time learning activity   *10–20 minutes*

The activities encourage listening with empathy and the kindness associated with empathy. Some suggested activities could be used in follow-up lessons.

Total time | *30–60 minutes (approx.)*

1 INTRODUCE THE THEME

Key points

- What is empathy?

- Everyone has feelings and we all appreciate people who understand our feelings and who are kind.

- In Circle Time we must all listen with empathy so that we can speak out in confidence and trust the circle.

- How can we show empathy in Circle Time? By listening attentively, responding with understanding and kindness, etc. Let the children make suggestions. Does anyone remember when someone showed empathy to them?

2 VOCABULARY

Use your usual methods for introducing new words.

The difficult words in the story are:

butter-fingers	–	*clumsy with hands*
crouching	–	*bending low*
glinting	–	*glittering; reflecting light*
costume	–	*clothes for a play; style of dress*
dress rehearsal	–	*practise a play wearing the costumes*
nudging	–	*touching slightly with elbow*
admitted	–	*confessed*
collection	–	*things gathered together*
swirl	–	*wavy pattern; twirling motion*
pattern	–	*design*
faceted	–	*many-sided*
swap	–	*barter; exchange*
rummaged	–	*searched thoroughly*
tempted	–	*enticed; invited/persuaded to*

3 THE STORY:

The Magic Bead

The Magic Bead

Millie stood alone, watching Laura and Amy swing the skipping rope in a big arch. The other girls took turns to skip, chanting, "jump high, jump low, jump high and out you go". Somehow Millie had never got the hang of skipping. She was no good at catching a ball either. Increasingly she was being left out of more and more games on Hillcrest Close, and Ellen Parker had started to call her mean names, such as "Miss Piggy butter-fingers", which made the other girls laugh.

"I don't care," Millie told herself.

Now it was Ellen Parker's turn to skip. She was very good at it.

"Look, you guys," Ellen yelled, as she began jumping high on one leg and crouching down to jump low.

Millie pretended to be looking at a bird in a tree. In the window of the house behind the tree she saw a shining silver fairy. The fairy had white wings, glinting with silver beads, and a long sparkly, silver gown. Diamonds twinkled in her long dark hair. The fairy actually waved at her.

"Look everyone, look," Millie shouted in excitement. "A silver fairy!"

"That's Azra in her ballet costume, silly," Laura said.

"Miss Piggy believes in fairies," said Ellen Parker.

Ellen continued her hop-jump chanting:

"Miss Piggy believes in fairies. Miss Piggy believes in fairies."

That became the new chant. Even Charlotte joined in, and the fairy had gone from the window. Millie turned away and went into her house feeling sad.

The next day at playtime Millie looked hard at Azra. She was in year six, and a prefect. Perhaps her wings were folded up beneath her long black hair? Millie watched as Azra helped a small boy who had fallen over. He was wailing hard and pointing at his knee. Azra patted this and he stopped crying immediately. *She's a good fairy*, Millie thought.

That afternoon Millie's class were led into the school hall. Year six were doing a dress rehearsal of their show. It began with five green elves dancing. Part-way through, Azra came on. The silver fairy was the only one who went right up on her toes. Millie thought Azra's dance was beautiful but she felt disappointed too. Perhaps her fairy dress and wings were only for the ballet after all.

The Story

Ellen Parker was nudging and whispering to another girl, who looked at Millie and giggled. Millie tried to ignore them and clapped the dancers as hard as she could. She blinked hard too so that Ellen would not see her tears.

After the dress rehearsal, as everyone was milling about, Azra came across to Millie and said "Hi. Did you like the show?"

Millie nodded shyly.

"I thought you were a real fairy in your window," she said.

Azra smiled down at her. "I am," she said. "Don't tell anyone though, will you? It's our secret." She winked at Millie, and Millie smiled.

"Why weren't you joining in the skipping last night?" Azra asked.

Azra had told Millie her fairy secret so Millie found herself telling Azra something she had not said to anyone else, not even Mum.

"I'm getting left out now," she said. "No one will play with me any more."

Azra looked at Millie with real sympathy and understanding. Gently she touched her arm.

"I'll think of something," she said.

After school that evening, Millie didn't go out to play. What was the point? Bored and lonely, she turned on the television.

"Look who's here," said her Mum, coming into the sitting room with Azra.

"Hi Millie," Azra said. "I've brought my bead tin from when I was your age. It's for you now."

It was a beautiful tin with a graceful picture of flower fairies on the lid. Inside was a collection of beads. There were twisty plastic beads in lollipop colours. There were gold, ceramic beads with swirly patterns. Best of all were the faceted red, amber and green glass beads, which reflected the light.

"Show the other girls and suggest that they get tins of beads too. The game is called "swapping beads", and that's what you do, try to get good swaps to make your collection even better."

"I have some smooth blue glass beads from a broken necklace," said Millie's Mum. "You can have those too."

"And this," said Azra. She rummaged in her bag and brought out a ball of purple tissue paper. She unwrapped a large round silver bead scattered with tiny "diamonds".

"Wow!" said Millie. The tiny diamonds looked like twinkling stars.

"This one is a magic bead," said Azra. "Never be tempted to swap it, Millie, it will keep you in the game. Now, off you go. Tell the girls to get tins of beads for a great new game."

"Swapping Beads" caught on. It was soon the latest craze and became called "Millie's Bead Game". Millie was in the thick of it. She loved the game and got very good. She had one of the nicest tins and one of the best collections. Everyone wanted to swap beads with Millie because they were secretly hoping they could swap for the twinkling silver bead. There was no other like it. They never succeeded. However many lovely beads they offered, Millie always refused that particular swap. She was determined to keep her magic bead forever.

4 TALKING ABOUT THE STORY

Did the children understand?

- Why did Millie go into her house feeling sad?

- Why did Millie think Azra was a **good** fairy?

- Why did Millie tell Azra about having no one to play with?

- What kind of beads did Millie have in her collection?

Points for discussion

- How did Azra show empathy for the little boy who fell over? And for Millie?

- What could you do if you were being left out? (Let the children suggest ideas.) Join a club. Make a special friend. Join in when a teacher is nearby. Find things you like doing on your own but let others join in when they want to.

- How can we show empathy for someone who is being left out?

5 THE CIRCLE TIME LEARNING ACTIVITY

1   Warm-up game

The Bead Game (resources needed: beads or counters, or coloured paper, in four different colours)

Give each child one red, one blue, one yellow and one green counter. The aim of the game is to end up with four counters of the same colour.

Go round the circle. Each child has a turn to ask for a swap of two beads (only). (E.g. I want to swap my red and green for a yellow and blue.) The children who wish to, and are able to swap, put up their hands for a swap. The child must try to choose someone who is not already a friend and shake hands on the friendly swap. Go round the circle a second time. (E.g. I want to swap my blue and blue for a yellow and yellow.) Who has ended up with four of the same colour? Well done. Finally you could go round the circle asking why each child chose the colour they did.

NB. To go round a large group of 30+ children might take too long. You could split the circle into smaller groups, or, in the one large group you could do one third of the circle each time (i.e. swap one; swap two; why did you chose that colour?).

2   Circle contribution

Kind deeds

Go round the circle and ask everyone to give an example of a kind deed.

Ask if anyone would like to thank someone else within the circle for a kindness they have shown during the term.

Go round the circle asking everyone to think of a kindness they could do that week.

3   Circle discussion

How can we help?/Inclusion

Go round the circle asking if anyone feels left out of anything. If a child volunteers an example, go round the circle for suggestions about how we can help. (Don't be surprised if no-one volunteers!)

People get left out or picked on for being different (e.g. wearing an unusual coat, or not being good at games). Go round the circle for examples of what might be picked on. Go round again for ideas about what we can do if you or someone else is picked on.

Talk about the value of inclusion. If everyone is made to feel welcome in a school or classroom or game or club or Circle Time, then you get a greater variety of people, which can be interesting. Also, this shows a spirit of kindness. You are open to new people and ideas, not closed and insecure.

Draw up class "rules" for an inclusive classroom.

4   Circle group work

Taking ideas from around the circle, make a list of "Ideas for an Inclusive Classroom".

The Magic Bead

Literacy Hour Three

Teacher's Notes

Theme Three: The value of **empathy** for characters in stories

Literacy Skills: Empathy helps us to understand the characters in the stories we read. In turn, reading helps us to develop empathy in real life, and to create sympathetic and realistic characters in our own stories.

▌ **Literacy Hour provides a regular time to explore character in fiction.**

Literacy Hour Plan

This five-part lesson plan is only a guide. Teachers are likely to add to or amend the learning activities which are suggested and may sometimes wish to substitute their own. For any part of the session they may wish to allow more or less time than that suggested.

1 Introduce the theme   *3–6 minutes*

Understanding characters in stories.

2 Vocabulary   *3–6 minutes*

Can the children produce synonyms, antonyms and sentences for the difficult words (which were covered in the Circle Time session)?

3 The story   *6 minutes*

This could be told or read by the children.

4 Talking about the story   *10–20 minutes*

The teacher uses some of the questions and discussion points given, stimulating the children to talk about the story as a narrative. This helps the children to develop a (literary) meta-language.

5 The Literacy Time learning activity   *10–20 minutes*

Some of the suggested activities help children's understanding of character in fiction. Some of the activities could be used in follow-up lessons.

| **Total time** | *30–60 minutes (approx.)* |

1 INTRODUCE THE THEME

Key points

- Why are the characters in a story so important? (We carry on reading because we are interested in the main character; we care about him/her.)

- In a story we see right inside a character – his or her thoughts and feelings. This can help us to understand ourselves and other real people.

2 VOCABULARY

Can you think of a word(s) that means the same as/the opposite to each of these? For each of the words, make up a sentence containing that word.

crouching	glinting
admitted	costume
swim	dress rehearsal
faceted	nudging
swap	collection
rummaged	tempted
butter-fingers	

3 THE STORY:

With younger children – ask them to use their own words to tell the story (*The Magic Bead*) which they listened to in Circle Time. With older children, go round the class having the children (re-) read the story out loud. Alternatively, give the children time to (re-) read the story to themselves.

The Magic Bead

4 TALKING ABOUT THE STORY

Did the children understand?

- Why did Millie say to herself "I don't care?" Was it true?

- What do you think Ellen was saying to the girl who looked at Millie and giggled?

- Do you think Azra was a real fairy? If not, why did she say she was?

Points for discussion

- What kind of person is Azra? (E.g. empathetic, kind, talented, intelligent.)

- What, for you, is the message of this story? (Examples: it hurts to be left out and called names; good people are kind to others who are hurt.) The children should understand that there is not just one correct answer.

5 THE LEARNING ACTIVITY

1   **Songs and Poems** (resources needed: poetry or song anthologies)

In pairs or small groups, find a poem or song which connects with the story. (It could be about kindness, jewellery/beads, dancing, fairies.) Ask some of the children to read their chosen poem or song.

2   **Story discussion**

How can we know when not to believe a character in a story? (Give examples: if they are a regular liar, like Pinocchio; or if they are trying to hide something.) You could also read out relevant extracts from stories and discuss these.

3   **Individual activity**

Positive and negative descriptions

Is the description of the fairy in the window positive/attractive? Is Azra a positive/kind person?
How would you describe the fairy in the window? What about Azra?

- Write a positive description of a good fairy.

- Write a negative description of a wicked witch.

- A character could look attractive but be mean. A character could look ugly but be kind. How would we know? (E.g. a beautiful but bad character might have cold eyes and never smile.) Get suggestions from the children.

- Write a description of a good-looking but mean character (e.g. the wicked queen) or of an ugly but kind character (e.g. the beast in *Beauty and the Beast*).

4   Group activity (resources needed: faceted card in different colours)

Remind the children that paying a compliment (kind words) counts as a kind deed. Each child is given a faceted card (use different colours) and a black pen. They must write down kind words or a kind deed, e.g. "You look nice today", or helping Mum to wash up.

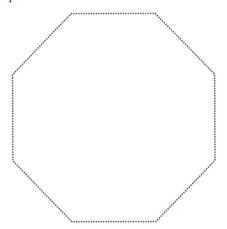

The children make a necklace by sticking their "kind bead" on a big sheet of paper on the wall which you have prepared.

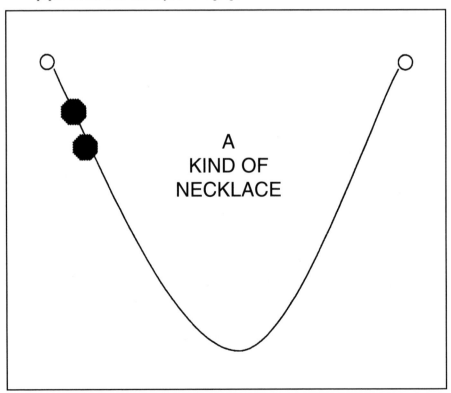

The Magic Bead
Assembly

Theme: Understanding and Kindness

Introduction

Pin the children's necklace of kind words and deeds on the wall at the front.

The assembly leader introduces the theme and talks about the importance of under-standing other people and of kindness, and draws attention to the necklace of kind words and deeds. Some of the children could read out their bead.

Story

Assembly leader

Our story today is about a girl called Azra who was understanding and helpful to a younger girl called Millie.

The assembly leader or a child reads the story – *The Magic Bead*

Poem or Song

You can choose a poem or a song, or both. Alternatively, you can have a child (or children) read the poems they chose or wrote in class and have one of the songs that were chosen. Select poems and songs which are relevant to the theme or which echo the story in some way.

Examples

Poem:

Swaps
Please Mrs Butler, by Allan Ahlberg, published by Puffin Books, 1984.

Song:

Think, think on these things
No. 38 in *Someone's Singing Lord* (2nd Edition), published by A&C Black, 2002.

Quiet reflection or prayer

For a universal, humanistic or multi-faith assembly:

Quiet reflection

The assembly leader says:
"Think of when someone was kind to us. How did we feel? (Pause) Let us remember when we were unkind to someone and feel sorry. (Pause) How can we be kind to someone today? (Pause)"

Or for Christian schools:

Prayer

Let us pray.

Dear Father,

Thank you for all your many kind gifts to us – our world, the people who care for us, our friends, our books, our games, our homes and our food. Help us to be kind too – to all those we meet each day and especially those who are hurt or sad.

Amen.

Chapter 4

Playing for Real

Circle Time Four

Teacher's Notes

Theme Four:	The value of **Compassion**
Circle Time Value:	Widening out from an empathetic understanding of others involves the development of compassion – loving care and concern. This is both an important element in our emotional development and a foundation for moral education (as concerned with principles of justice and care).

Circle Time provides a forum in which children can be encouraged to care about others in the circle (and thus beyond it).

Circle Time Plan

This five-part lesson plan is only a guide. Teachers are likely to add to or amend the learning activities which are suggested and may sometimes wish to substitute their own. For any part of the session they may wish to allow more or less time than that suggested.

1 Introduce the theme *3–6 minutes*

What is **compassion**? How can we show compassion in Circle Time?

2 Vocabulary *3–6 minutes*

The teacher ensures that the children understand the words given.

3 The story *6 minutes*

The teacher shows the illustration and reads the story.

4 Talking about the story *10–20 minutes*

The teacher uses some of the questions and discussion points given, stimulating the children to talk about the story/theme.

5 The Circle Time learning activity *10–20 minutes*

These activities encourage caring behaviour in and beyond Circle Time. Some suggested activities could be used in follow-up lessons.

Total time *30–60 minutes (approx.)*

1 INTRODUCE THE THEME

Key points

- Compassion means feeling sorry with understanding for people who are hurt or ill or in some kind of bad situation.

- Distinguish compassionate action from interfering, and compassion from patronisation. (Compassion does not let you feel "superior" to the other person.)

- It is easier to be kind when we feel compassion.

2 VOCABULARY

Use your usual methods for introducing new words.

The difficult words in the story are:

prompter	–	*person telling the next words*
dread	–	*fear and awe*
exasperation	–	*annoyance*
self-conscious	–	*aware of oneself; shy and nervous*
desperate	–	*despairing*
stilted	–	*stiff in speech or manner*
documentary	–	*programme dealing with real life*
drought	–	*long spell of dry weather*
ruined	–	*spoiled*
listless	–	*lacking in energy*
plight	–	*distressing state*
OXFAM	–	*a charity which helps developing countries*

Playing for Real

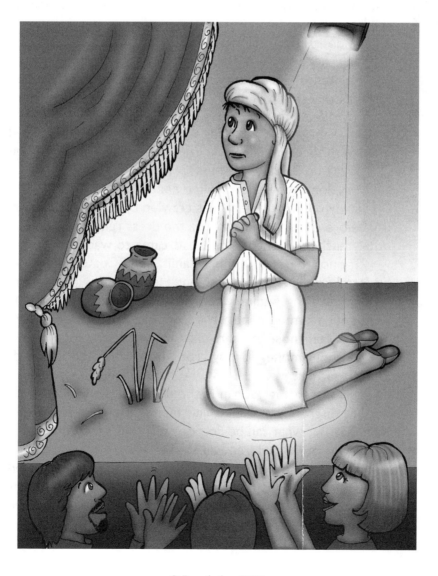

Playing for Real

Except for Ranjit, the children sat up straight, wanting to be picked.

"Ranjit, you can be Farmer Sohan," said Miss Coates. "Don't look so horrified, dear. It's time you had a speaking part."

In previous school plays, Ranjit had non-speaking parts. He had been a member of a crowd and, in the last play, a dead body, which had suited him just fine.

"B … b … but I'll s … spoil it," he blurted out. Ranjit's slight stammer was worse when he was anxious, and a couple of the children sniggered.

"I'll do it, Miss," Mark offered.

Ranjit felt a surge of hope.

"Nonsense," said Miss Coates, sharply. "You can be Anil, the Farmer's oldest son."

Rehearsals began the following week. Ranjit lived in dread of them. They were sheer misery. At first he had spoken his lines too quietly.

"Speak up Ranjit," said Miss Coates.

"No, don't shout, dear," came next.

Slowly the miserable weeks crawled by until, at last, it was the day before the play and time for the dress rehearsal. Some of the other teachers, including the Head, came to watch.

"Try not to be so wooden, Ranjit," Miss Coates said. Ranjit felt his face burn with embarrassment. He felt as low as a worm.

That evening Ranjit watched the television with his Mum. It was about a farmer in India. His crops had been ruined by drought. Without rain, most had shrivelled up and died.

"Without money for my crops, how can I feed my children?" said the farmer.

"Just like Farmer Sohan in the play," said Ranjit.

"It's disgraceful," said Ranjit's Mum. "The grain is worth more than that. But what can he do, poor man? He's forced to take what he can get or his children will starve."

In bed, that night, Ranjit couldn't get to sleep. He tossed and turned restlessly, his mind on the play. He was sure to stammer in front of the whole school. Parents were invited too, and his Mum would be disappointed and embarrassed by his "wooden" performance and his stammer.

The Story

Ranjit was tired the next morning and wished he could stay in bed, but, all too soon he found himself at school, dressed as Farmer Sohan, and waiting helplessly in the wings for the dreaded moment when he must move out onto the stage.

When he did so, he saw that the school hall was packed. Rows of upturned faces were staring at him and Ranjit froze.

"Rain. Rain. If only it would rain," hissed the prompter.

Ranjit plunged into his first speech – a long plea for rain. Perhaps his own helpless feelings made the play real, but miraculously he became Farmer Sohan, desperate to save his crops. The audience faded, and the farmer pleaded for the rain. Ranjit's stammer completely disappeared. He held the audience enthralled. He wanted them to understand his despair as his children grew hungry and sick. At the end of the play, a thunderous applause broke out.

"Step forward, Ranjit," Miss Coates called from the wings. When he did so, the audience rose in a standing ovation.

After that, Ranjit loved doing plays, but when he left school, he decided to work for OXFAM. He never forgot Farmer Sohan. He had felt his helplessness, and he knew that to feel helpless about feeding your hungry children was the worse feeling a person could have.

4 TALKING ABOUT THE STORY

Did the children understand?

- Why did Ranjit **not** want to have a speaking part?

- What do you think Miss Coates meant when she said "Try not to be so wooden, Ranjit"?

- What did the farmer in the documentary have in common with the farmer in the school play?

- How do we know that the audience enjoyed Ranjit's performance in the play?

Points for discussion

- How can we help someone with a stammer? (Don't complete their sentence or make them self-conscious about their stammer.)

- Go round the circle and ask: "What things that you see on the television make you feel sorry for the people involved?"

- Do the children know about OXFAM?

5 THE CIRCLE TIME LEARNING ACTIVITY

1 Warm-up game

Let the children take turns to mime a helping action, e.g. washing up or sweeping the floor. The other children must guess the action.

2 Circle contribution

Kind/unkind words and deeds

Go round the circle for kind words (e.g. peace, thanks, love, praise). Go round the circle for unkind words (e.g. bully, mean, cruel, selfish). Go round the circle for kind deeds (e.g. pay a compliment, praise someone, help someone). Go round the circle for unkind deeds (e.g. name-calling, stealing).

Each child can then be given a copy of the photocopiable page (page 60). They can fill in the "word" and "deed" blanks, choosing the "circle examples" which they liked best.

3 Circle discussion

Past and present

Go round the circle and ask the children to share one kind deed which they have already done (e.g. in the past week). Discuss why it was kind.

Go round the circle and ask the children to tell one kind deed which they plan to do in the future (e.g. in the coming week). Discuss these suggestions.

Give examples of things people do for others (e.g. charity shops, fund-raising, visiting, cards/letters/toys to hospitals).

4   Circle group work

Go round the circle and ask for ideas about a community or group project that the children could do (emphasise that these suggestions must be practical), e.g. bring in unwanted goods/toys from home to give to the local charity shop; make and send cards to a school member who is off sick. Have some discussion about each suggestion and write down all those that are practical. (Some suggestions may come up more than once, which is fine.)

Go round the circle for each child to make a point in support of one of the suggestions on the list (not their own). Take a vote, and subsequently assist the children to carry out their project.

WORDS	
KIND	**UNKIND**
• Thanks	• Silly
•	•
•	•
•	•

DEEDS	
KIND	**UNKIND**
• Pay a compliment	• Pick on someone
•	•
•	•
•	•

Playing for Real

Literacy Hour Four

Teacher's Notes

Theme Four: The value of **Caring about the "character"**

Literacy Skills: We enjoy stories when we care about the characters, and we strengthen our own good values (our capacity to care in real life) through this involvement with literature.

> Literacy Hour provides a regular time in which children can engage with the characters in plays and stories to develop a greater compassion for "real-life" support of others.

Literacy Hour Plan

This five-part lesson plan is only a guide. Teachers are likely to add to or amend the learning activities which are suggested and may sometimes wish to substitute their own. For any part of the session they may wish to allow more or less time than that suggested.

1 Introduce the theme *3–6 minutes*

We will explore how and why we care about what happens to the character in a story. We identify with the hero/heroine. We would (usually) be less interested in a story if we didn't care about the character.

2 Vocabulary *3–6 minutes*

Can the children produce synonyms, antonyms and sentences for the difficult words (which were covered in the Circle Time session)?

3 The story *6 minutes*

This could be told or read by the children.

4 Talking about the story *10–20 minutes*

The teacher uses some of the questions and discussion points given, stimulating the children to talk about the story as a narrative. This helps the children to develop a (literary) meta-language.

5 The Literacy Time learning activity *10–20 minutes*

Some of the suggested "literacy" activities encourage group work as a positive enhancement of the Circle Time skills and values. Some of the activities could be used in follow-up lessons.

| **Total time** | *30–60 minutes (approx.)* |

1 INTRODUCE THE THEME

Key points

- Do you feel sorry for Ranjit in the story? When/why?

- What other characters in a story have stirred your compassion?

2 VOCABULARY

Can you think of a word(s) that means the same as/the opposite to each of these? For each off the words, make up a sentence containing that word.

indifferently

anxiety

plunge

enthralled

embarrassment

plea

ovation

3 THE STORY:

With younger children – ask them to use their own words to tell the story (*Playing for Real*) which they listened to in Circle Time. With older children, go round the class having the children (re-) read the story out loud. Alternatively, give the children time to (re-) read the story to themselves.

Playing for Real

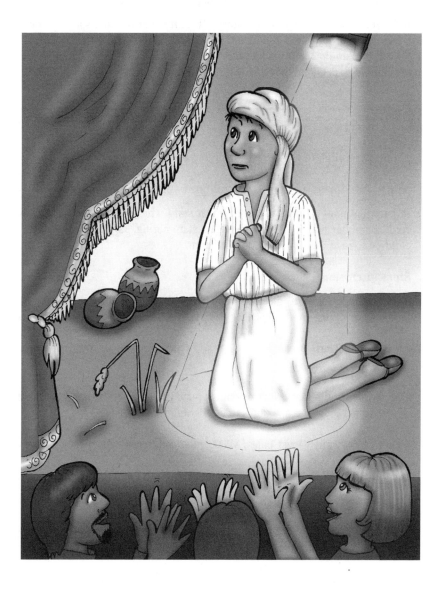

4   TALKING ABOUT THE STORY

Did the children understand?

- Why was having this part (the farmer) worse than the parts which Ranjit had in previous school plays?

- Why was Ranjit interested in the documentary?

- Why did Ranjit lose his self-consciousness and his stammer in his performance in the play?

Points for discussion

- Do you think an experience now could influence your choice of career after school?

- What, for you, is the message of this story? (E.g. It is not fair that some children in the world are starving; or, you can understand and sympathise with someone's feelings if you have felt a similar emotion; or, don't pick on someone who stammers, etc.) The children should understand that there is not just one correct answer.

5   THE LEARNING ACTIVITY

The activities link to the story through the use of poetry.

1   **Songs and Stories** (resources needed: poetry or song anthologies)

In pairs or small groups, find a poem or song which connects with the story. (It could be about acting, hunger, poverty, stammering, farming.) Ask some of the children to read their chosen song or poem.

2   **Story discussion**

Take the opportunity to discuss the inequalities of world trade with the children. Perhaps you could invite a speaker from OXFAM to discuss OXFAM's work.

3   **Individual activity**

Play writing

The children could make the story into a play, i.e. the story of Ranjit having the part of the farmer and how he comes to do a good performance.

Characters: Ranjit, Miss Coates, Mark, other children, Head teacher, Ranjit's Mum.

Scenes: Ranjit picked for the part; the rehearsals; the dress rehearsal; watching the documentary with his Mum; the performance and standing ovations.

4   **Group Activity**

Choose a play and have a play reading session.

- First the children read their part as though they feel very self-conscious.

- A pause while the children study their part.

- Second the children read their part trying to "be" that character and feel as the character feels.

Playing for Real
Assembly

Theme: Compassion

Introduction
The assembly leader introduces the theme and talks about compassion for those in trouble and those less fortunate.

Story
Assembly leader:

Our story today is about Ranjit, who discovers how terrible it would be not to have food for your children. His compassion shines in his acting and influences what career he chooses later in his life.

The assembly leader or a child reads the story – *Playing for Real*

Poem or Song
You can choose a poem or a song, or both. Select poems and songs which are relevant to the theme or which echo the story in some way.

Examples

Poem:

Abou Ben Adhem, by Leigh Hunt
Page 216 in *The Poetry Book*, published by Dolphin Paperback, 1999.

Song:

Because you care
No. 31 in *Every Colour Under The Sun*, published by Ward Lock Educational Co. Ltd, 1983.

Quiet reflection or prayer
For a universal, humanistic or multi-faith assembly:

Quiet reflection

The assembly leader says:
Think for a moment of how terrible it would be to be hungry and poor with too little food. (Pause) Think of those who are less fortunate than we are. (Pause) Let us resolve to do something to help them, and think what we could do. (Pause)

Or for Christian schools:

Prayer

Let us pray.

Heavenly Father,
Thank you for our daily bread. Bless those who are hungry today and help us to find ways to help those who are less fortunate than we are.

Amen.

Chapter 5

The Power of a Smile

Circle Time Five

Teacher's Notes

Theme Five: The value of **Relationship**

Circle Time Value: The self connects with the other in relationship. Through learning to share with, respect, love and trust the "other" we develop the special relationships of family and friends.

> Circle Time provides a forum in which each child can give and receive appreciation and trust. The circle provides a kind of family.

Circle Time Plan

This five-part lesson plan is only a guide. Teachers are likely to add to or amend the learning activities which are suggested and may sometimes wish to substitute their own. For any part of the session they may wish to allow more or less time than that suggested.

1 Introduce the theme   *3–6 minutes*

What is a **family**? Why is family important? (There are many kinds of family.) What is a friend? Why is friendship important?

2 Vocabulary   *3–6 minutes*

The teacher ensures that the children understand the words given.

3 The story   *6 minutes*

The teacher shows the illustration and reads the story.

4 Talking about the story   *10–20 minutes*

The teacher uses some of the questions and discussion points given, stimulating the children to talk about the story/theme.

5 The Circle Time learning activity   *10–20 minutes*

These activities encourage mutual appreciation and trust. Some suggested activities could be used in follow-up lessons.

Total time *30–60 minutes (approx.)*

1 INTRODUCE THE THEME

Key points

- We all need and value friends to play and work with.

- In Circle Time we must treat all members of the circle as friends, i.e. with appreciation and trust.

2 VOCABULARY

Use your usual methods for introducing new words.

The difficult words in the story are:

cradling	–	holding and rocking as in a cradle
swap	–	exchange
ignored	–	excluded; gave no attention to someone
pretended	–	made believe, as in a play
cute	–	appealing
peep	–	take a quick look
deliberately	–	on purpose
colic	–	pains inside
concentrate	–	give all attention; focus
to rock	–	to sway gently
fault	–	error
enough	–	sufficient
copy	–	imitate
chuckle	–	soft laughter

3 THE STORY:

The Power of a Smile

The Power of a Smile

Imani watched as they wheeled Mum away. She saw Dad almost running to keep up with the hospital trolley but Imani had to wait in the waiting room with a nurse. She waited and waited. She was wondering if Mum and Dad had forgotten about her when another nurse came in.

"You've got a lovely baby brother my dear," the nurse said.

"Oh no," said Imani, crossly. "I said I wanted a sister."

"Well, come and see," said the nurse. "He's beautiful."

Mum was in bed cradling the tiny baby in her arms, and Dad was sitting near and gazing at them. Mum and Dad looked up and smiled at Imani, who went and stared at the baby. He wasn't beautiful at all. He was wrinkled and bald.

"Isn't he beautiful?" said Mum.

"No," said Imani. "Honestly, he isn't. Now a sister probably would be. Can't you swap?"

This made Mum and Dad laugh, and Imani felt more cross than ever.

"Well, don't expect me to have anything to do with a brother, that's all," she said.

A few days later Mum came home with the baby, and as the weeks went by Imani kept to her word. She ignored her new brother. She pretended he wasn't there.

"Look Imani," Mum would say. "He's staring at the light," or "Look how cute he looks in his blue sailor suit."

"I'm not interested," Imani said.

She hid behind the sofa when he was out of his Moses basket, though secretly she sometimes wanted to peep.

Everyone made a ridiculous fuss of the baby and brought him presents that he was too young to play with. Even Imani's favourite Aunty brought him a soft brown teddy bear, which Imani would have liked to have for herself. Aunty Sonia usually played great games with Imani but this time she was too busy holding the baby and taking a turn to give him his bottle. She didn't even notice when Imani went behind the sofa and played by herself.

One day Mum and Dad gave Imani a parcel with a gift tag that said, "From your brother". Imani opened it. She was pleased with her new trainers but she knew that they were really from Mum and Dad. She wasn't a little kid. She knew that a small baby couldn't really buy a present.

"Thank you Mum and thank you Dad," she said, deliberately leaving out her brother. "They're cool."

Imani hated the baby's crying noise. It was an awful sound. It was worse than squeaky chalk on a blackboard. You just wanted him to shut up, which he did, like magic, when Mum or Dad gave him his bottle. After a while he began to cry all evening, even after his bottle. The noise went right through Imani until she couldn't even think.

"It's colic, poor little thing," said Mum.

"He just likes to make a racket," Imani said. "Noisy boy!"

One evening Imani was trying to do her homework. The teacher had said she should write about a place that she liked. Imani liked the park. She wrote about it having trees, flowers, swings and a lake, but when the baby began to wail she just couldn't concentrate any more. He was in his basket and Mum had gone to answer the phone. In order to stop the awful crying, Imani thought that she would rock the basket without looking in.

Imani began to rock the cradle and the crying gradually stopped. She peeped in the cot, just to see if the baby had fallen asleep. The baby stared back at her, his eyes growing big. He gave her a sudden happy smile. He looked so delighted to see her that Imani couldn't help herself. She smiled back.

"He's smiling," Mum said, coming in behind Imani. She sounded excited.

"Imani, you got Joseph's first smile!" Imani held out her hand and Joseph grasped one of her fingers. He held it and waved it about.

"He's shaking hands in his own way," Mum said.

The baby looked much better than before. His skin was smooth as silk and his eyes were big and bright.

"He looks nice, now," Imani said, surprised.

After that, Imani went back to her homework, but she found that she was stuck. Joseph wasn't crying now so it wasn't his fault. She just couldn't think what else to write.

"Quack, quelsh," said Joseph. The sound made Imani think of the ducks on the lake. She wrote about them and about swans, squirrels and dogs.

"Peep plob po peep," burbled Joseph. It sounded as though he was trying to say "people". That gave Imani another idea. She wrote about the things people did in the park – swinging, playing ball, feeding the ducks, walking dogs. Thanks to Joseph, she soon finished her homework. She closed her exercise book and went back to her brother. He tried to copy the sounds she made.

"I'm teaching him to talk," she said to Mum.

Imani soon loved her little brother very much. She became a good big sister. She enjoyed making him chuckle and it wasn't long before he could walk. Imani was even able to dress him up in things from her dressing-up box.

One day Mum said, "Imani, I've something tell you. I'm going to have another baby quite soon."

Imani thought for a moment.

"Good," she said. "And Mum, honestly, this time I don't mind which kind you have."

As it happens, Mum had twins, a boy and a girl.

4 ∎ TALKING ABOUT THE STORY

Did the children understand?

- Why did Mum and Dad laugh when Imani suggested that they swapped the new baby?

- Why did Mum and Dad give Imani a present from the baby?

- Why did Imani rock the cradle?

- Why, in the end, didn't Imani mind if Mum's next baby was a boy or a girl?

Points for discussion

- Discuss the feelings of jealousy and envy. How do these emotions "feel"? How might they make you behave?

- How can we keep negative feelings out of Circle Time?

5 ∎ THE CIRCLE TIME LEARNING ACTIVITY

1   Warm-up game

The Introduction Game

The first child leaves his seat in the circle and walks across the circle to another child he doesn't usually play with. He introduces himself, smiling. (E.g. "Hi. I'm Joseph. It's good to meet you.") The seated child gets up, shakes hands and introduces herself. (E.g. "Hi. I'm Helen. It's good to meet you too.") Joseph takes Helen's seat. Helen crosses the circle and repeats the process until everyone has had a turn.

2   Circle contribution

Making friends

How can we make Circle Time like a family circle? Go round the circle asking everyone to say one quality they like in their friends. How can we make new friends? Go round the circle for suggestions.

3   Circle discussion

Has anyone had a new baby brother or sister? What do they feel about him/her? This can lead into a discussion about jealousy and/or looking after younger children.

4   Circle group work

How should we treat children who are younger than we are? Perhaps the teacher can arrange with a colleague who has a younger class to do some "children swaps". The older ones could teach the younger ones an agreed learning "game".

The Power of a Smile

Literacy Hour Five

Teacher's Notes

Theme Five: The value of **Relationship**

Literacy Skills: The social skills associated with making friends enable children to cooperate in such activities as play-acting. Literature contributes by increasing our understanding of relationship.

> **Literacy Hour provides a regular time in which children can work together on plays and stories. They can share the experience of this rich world of characters and their relationships.**

Literacy Hour Plan

This five-part lesson plan is only a guide. Teachers are likely to add to or amend the learning activities which are suggested and may sometimes wish to substitute their own. For any part of the session they may wish to allow more or less time than that suggested.

1 Introduce the theme *3–6 minutes*

What good and bad families or friends can we remember from stories?

2 Vocabulary *3–6 minutes*

Can the children produce synonyms, antonyms and sentences for the difficult words (which were covered in the Circle Time session)?

3 The story *6 minutes*

This could be told or read by the children.

4 Talking about the story *10–20 minutes*

The teacher uses some of the questions and discussion points given, stimulating the children to talk about the story as a narrative. This helps the children to develop a (literary) meta-language.

5 The Literacy Time learning activity *10–20 minutes*

Some of the suggested "literacy" activities encourage group work as a positive enhancement of the Circle Time skills and values. Some of the activities could be used in follow-up lessons.

| **Total time** | *30–60 minutes (approx.)* |

1 INTRODUCE THE THEME

Key points

- What makes a good friend? What can destroy a friendship?

- When are siblings (brothers and sisters) also friends?

2 VOCABULARY

Can you think of a word(s) that means the same as/the opposite to each of these? For each of the words, make up a sentence containing that word.

ignored	cute
pretend	(to) rock
peep	fault
deliberately	chuckle
concentrate	colic
enough	swap
copy	twins
cradling	

3 THE STORY:

With younger children – ask them to use their own words to tell the story (*The Power of a Smile*) which they listened to in Circle Time. With older children, go round the class having the children (re-) read the story out loud. Alternatively, give the children time to (re-) read the story to themselves.

The Power of a Smile

4 TALKING ABOUT THE STORY

Did the children understand?

- How do we know that Imani was jealous of the new baby?

- What might a mother say instead of "poor little thing"? (E.g. poor little duck; poor little mite (old fashioned).)

Points for discussion

- Why do babies smile at people and copy the sounds they make?

- Why are smiles important?

- What, for you, is the message in this story? What could it be? (E.g. Smiles are friendly. Human beings/babies are **social**. Jealousy feels bad; friendship feels good.) The children should understand that there is not just one correct answer.

5 THE LEARNING ACTIVITY

1   **Songs and Poems** (resources needed: poetry or song anthologies)

In pairs or small groups, find a poem or song which connects with the story. (It could be about families, friends, smiles or jealousy.) Ask some of the children to read their poem or song.

2   **Story discussion**

You could take the opportunity to raise the sensitive issue of "family" – aim to show that there are many kinds of family. It is lucky to have a good family, where everyone loves and helps each other. When you grow up, how would you like to live?

3   **Individual activity**

A favourite place

Ask the children to write their own description of "A Place That You Like". (E.g. sights, sounds, smells, activities – people/creatures. What else?)
They should choose a place they would like to take a friend.

4   **Group activity**

Pair play

- In pairs, let the children read their description of "A Place that I Like" to each other. Each child tries to visualise (see) the place which their partner is describing.

- Working in pairs, write a short scene (from a play) in which two children are making friends. (Some of these could be read or acted out to the whole class.)

The Power of a Smile

Assembly

Theme: Friendship: Appreciation and Trust

Introduction

The assembly leader introduces the theme and talks about the importance of friends. What makes a good friend?

Story

Assembly leader:

Our story today is about Imani, a girl who overcomes her jealousy to make friends with her new baby brother. The friendship begins with the baby's warm smile.

The assembly leader or a child reads the story – *The Power of a Smile*.

Poem or Song

You can choose a poem or a song, or both. Alternatively, you can have a child (or children) read the poems they chose or wrote in class and have one of the songs that were chosen. Select poems and songs which are relevant to the theme or which echo the story in some way. One or two of the small "scenes" could also be "performed".

Examples

Poem:

I had no friends at all, by John Kitching
Page 18 in *A Very First Poetry Book*, published by Oxford University Press, 1984.

Song:

It's a great, great shame
No. 44 in *Every Colour Under The Sun*, published by Ward Lock Educational Co. Ltd, 1983.

Quiet reflection or prayer

For a universal, humanistic or multi-faith assembly:

Quiet reflection

The assembly leader says:

Think of a friend. Appreciate your friend for a moment – thinking of what you like about them. (Pause) Think, too, about the power of a smile. (Pause) Resolve to smile at someone today. (Pause) Think about lonely people and how to befriend someone like that. (Pause)

Or for Christian schools:

Prayer

Let us pray.

Dear God,
Thank you for friends and for smiles. Please help me to be a good friend. Help us all to be friendly and to befriend those without friends. Give your strength to those who are lonely today.

Amen.

Chapter 6

The Mystery of the Missing Fish

Circle Time Six

Teacher's Notes

Theme Six: The value of **Cooperation**

Circle Time Value: As the children develop empathy and compassion and build social skills in family relationships and friendships, they are increasingly able to cooperate with others. Group cooperation is an important Circle Time value.

Circle Time provides a forum in which the children increasingly expect to cooperate with the Circle Time group and can practise the skills inherent in such cooperation.

Circle Time Plan

This five-part lesson plan is only a guide. Teachers are likely to add to or amend the learning activities which are suggested and may sometimes wish to substitute their own. For any part of the session they may wish to allow more or less time than that suggested.

1 Introduce the theme *3–6 minutes*

What is **cooperation**? How can we help each other to cooperate in Circle Time?

2 Vocabulary *3–6 minutes*

The teacher ensures that the children understand the words given.

3 The story *6 minutes*

The teacher shows the illustration and reads the story.

4 Talking about the story *10–20 minutes*

The teacher uses some of the questions and discussion points given, stimulating the children to talk about the story/theme.

5 The Circle Time learning activity *10–20 minutes*

These activities require value and provide practice in Circle Time Group work/cooperation. Some suggested activities could be used in follow-up lessons.

| **Total time** | *30–60 minutes (approx.)* |

1 INTRODUCE THE THEME

Key points

- We cooperate when we help each other by doing something **together**. (How is this different from simply "helping"?)

- Sometimes we cooperate in pairs (i.e. with one other person). Sometimes we cooperate in a whole group.

- Give examples of cooperating in pairs. (E.g. washing and drying the dishes; holding down the paper on a parcel while the other person sticks on the sticky tape.) Go round the circle asking the children to given an example of their own.

2 VOCABULARY

Use your usual methods for introducing new words.

The difficult words in the story are:

sign/signing	–	speaking with gestures
lip-read	–	understand spoken words from movement of speaker's lips
cascaded	–	fell like a waterfall
squatting	–	sitting on heels
twirling	–	swirling movement
flashing	–	on/off light
disappeared	–	vanished
mystery	–	secret, inexplicable thing
homesick	–	missing home
isolated	–	lonely
flinch	–	draw back, wince
ornamental	–	decorative
heron	–	a type of bird
kiln	–	an oven to bake clay pots in

3 THE STORY:

The Mystery of the Missing Fish

The Mystery of the Missing Fish

Megan was walking round the gardens by herself. She had been at the Guide camp for only a few days but already she felt lonely. The other girls didn't know how to sign. Sometimes they remembered to face Megan, so that she could lip-read, but often they forgot.

Megan came to a large fish pond and stopped to look. At the far end a fountain cascaded sparks of bright water. At the near end Megan saw a big green toad squatting on one of the lily pads. He seemed to stare at her with unblinking eyes. She watched gold and silver fish darting through the water, just missing each other in a twirling, flashing dance.

Mrs Cheshire, who ran the camp, joined her at the pond. Together they watched the fish. Mrs Cheshire was the only other person at the camp who knew sign language.

"Hi Megan," she signed, "why are you here, all by yourself?"

"I'm not good at singing, Mrs Cheshire," Megan signed. "And I don't really enjoy rounders."

"What do you like, dear?" Mrs Cheshire asked her.

"I like walking," signed Megan. "Looking at creatures and flowers."

"Me too," signed Mrs Cheshire.

She threw some pellets into the pond and they watched the fish rise in a sudden swirling mass to snap up the food.

"Some of my biggest fish have disappeared," Mrs Cheshire told Megan. "It's a complete mystery. I'm really worried about it."

Megan could see the frown on Mrs Cheshire's face. They walked slowly back to the house.

"Well, my dear," signed Mrs Cheshire, "try to think of a camp project that you would enjoy. Something you could do with some of the other girls."

As the week went by, Megan spent more and more time alone. However hard she tried, she could not think of a project the others would want to join in. Megan felt useless.

She longed to be back with her mother and father and brother, all of whom, though hearing, could sign almost as well as she could herself. By the end of the first week she felt very homesick. That night she shed a few quiet tears. One week had passed but there were still three whole weeks to get through before she could go home.

She fell asleep at last and next morning she woke to a particularly sunny day. Mrs Cheshire decided that they would all have lunch in the garden. Everyone helped to carry out plates, glasses and food. Megan enjoyed this. It was something she could join in and the three other girls in her dormitory, Tyesha, Jill and Anna, saved her a seat at their table. They started out by talking to her face-on, and she replied in her thick, rusty voice. This was much less easy for her than signing would have been, but she was happy to join in. Gradually, however, the three girls were chatting only to each other. Megan was left to follow as best she could. She could make out that they wanted to buy a thank-you gift for Mrs Cheshire but had spent nearly all their money. After that they talked about their choir practice. Tired of twisting her head from one to the other, Megan gave up and walked over to the pond. She frightened a heron, who flapped away. *Even the birds fly away from me*, she thought, feeling isolated again and a bit sorry for herself.

As though in sympathy with Megan's feelings, the blue sky darkened and emptied a sudden summer storm over the open-air lunch. Torrents of rain hurtled down.

Most of the girls ran to the house, but Megan's table was at the farthest end, near the pond and the summerhouse. She and the three girls took shelter there. They watched the storm rage outside, the rain making huge ripples on the pond. Lightning lit the sky. Megan couldn't hear the thunder but she could see the other girls flinch with fear and guessed that it was crashing directly above.

Tyesha was very upset. Her hands went up to her face and she was trembling. *The sound must be very alarming*, Megan thought. She patted Tyesha's shoulder, trying to reassure her. Tyesha moved closer to Megan, and grasped her arm when the wind blew open the summerhouse door. Rain and cold air swirled in. Megan re-latched the door and returned to Tyesha. She put an arm round Tyesha's shoulders until the storm died away.

Later, in their dormitory, the girls talked about the dreadful thunder and Megan told them about the heron she had seen before it began.

"We have an ornamental heron at the edge of our pond at home," Tyesha said, taking care to face Megan as she spoke. "That keeps the real herons away. Otherwise they eat the fish."

"Of course!" exclaimed Megan. "I bet that heron I saw is eating Mrs Cheshire's fish!"

"Have some gone missing then?" asked Anna.

Megan nodded. She smiled as an idea, bright as the lightning, flashed into her mind.

"Why don't we make a clay heron in the pottery class?" she said. "A gift for Mrs Cheshire."

"What a brilliant idea!" Jill said.

"We'll keep it a secret," said Anna, "until he's made."

Mrs Tate, the art teacher, was pleased to help the girls with their heron project. They found a picture of a heron in a library book and copied its long legs, long neck and long beak. They glazed it a pale grey colour and Mrs Tate fired it in the kiln. Megan enjoyed working with Tyesha, Jill and Anna. They asked her to teach them sign language and she enjoyed that even more. Tyesha, in particular, was soon very good at it.

Mrs Cheshire was delighted with her heron. The four girls helped her to place it by the pond. Mrs Cheshire asked Megan and her friends to feed the fish every day after that.

Megan soon knew the different shapes and colours of the fish and grew fond of each one. She was happy that they were now safe.

The final day came more quickly than Megan had expected, and though she was glad to be going home, she was sorry too.

"Goodbye Megan," Tyesha signed, as Megan was about to climb into her parents' car. "I'll write to you, shall I?"

Megan smiled and quickly scribbled her address. A week later she was delighted to receive her first letter from Tyesha. It had a picture of a heron on the front.

4 TALKING ABOUT THE STORY

Did the children understand?

- Why did Megan feel lonely at first?
- What kind of project did Megan have to think up?
- Why were there some missing fish?
- Why wasn't Megan frightened of the thunder?

Points for discussion

- Why is it good to cooperate? (Some tasks need more than one person. Cooperation builds good relationships and friendships.)
- Why should we face a deaf person when we talk together?
- Why is learning sign language a good idea?
- Megan taught the other three girls how to use sign language. Is **teaching** a good example of cooperation?

5 THE CIRCLE TIME LEARNING ACTIVITY

1 Warm-up game

Fish and Toads

- Make a pair with a child sitting next to you. Each pair has to decide who will be a fish and who will be a toad.
- All fish raise their hands.
- One child chooses a fish at the opposite side of the circle. The two must "swim" to the other's chair, gliding/twirling round inside the circle without bumping into each other. Other pairs have a try.
- Next, build up the numbers. How many pairs before bumps cannot be avoided?
- Now the toads raise their hands.
- Opposite-side toads must squat jump – weaving in and out of the chairs to take their partner's chair – without bumping (i.e. by going round in the same direction!). Now other pairs of toads can try.
- How many pairs could go round at the same time?

2 Circle contribution

Go round the circle asking the children to:

- Give an example of a collaborative project they have been involved with.

- Give a suggestion of a class collaborative project that they would like to do.

3   Circle discussion

- Has anyone here ever been homesick? (The children can describe their experience. Where were they? How did they feel? Why? etc.)

- Has anyone here ever felt lonely or isolated? (The children can also talk about these experiences.)

- Does anyone ever feel isolated in the class or playground? (What can we all do to help?)

4   Circle group work

The teacher will need to have learned some sign language: how to say "Hi" or "Hello", "What is your name?", "How are you?", "My name is _____". First show the group how to sign "Hello. How are you?" Each child signs this to the next child round the circle.

Next show the signs for "What is your name?" and "My name is _____".

Start by asking the child on your left "What is your name?" The child signs, "My name is _____". S/he then asks the next child, "What is your name?" The child replies and then turns to repeat the process round the circle.

After this, get the children to cast the story as a play – deciding on the following parts (these must be group decisions):

Megan	Jill
The Toad	The Heron
Mrs Cheshire	Mrs Tate
Tyesha	Megan's Mum
Anna	Megan's Dad

Some of the children are cast as fishes and some are other girls. The children role-play the story in the centre of the circle. Give them time to discuss their scenes and to work out the sequence of scenes. Examples:

1   Megan at the Pond

The toad squats, making toad noises. Fishes swirl and dance – before sitting again. Mrs Cheshire comes. She and Meg (pretend to) sign.

2   The Outdoor Lunch

Other children helping to set the tables. The four girls sit at their table chatting.

Megan sees the Heron.

The sudden storm – everyone running for shelter.

3   In the Summer House

The girls in the storm.

4   In the Dormitory

The girls and the Pot Heron idea.

5   In the Pottery Class

Making the heron.

6   At the Pond

The four girls and Mrs Cheshire placing the heron.

7   Going Home

Megan's Mum and Dad arrive in the car. Tyesha signs to Megan – gets her address.

8   Receiving the Letter

Megan receives her letter/card from Tyesha.

The Mystery of the Missing Fish

Literacy Hour Six

Teacher's Notes

Theme Six: The value of **Cooperation**

Literacy Skills: "Literacy" activities require cooperation; discussion and debate, for example. "Oracy" skills are underpinned by the values of cooperative participation. Plays are also a good example of a collaborative project.

| Literacy Hour provides a regular time in which these group-based "oracy" skills can be practised.

Literacy Hour Plan

This five-part lesson plan is only a guide. Teachers are likely to add to or amend the learning activities which are suggested and may sometimes wish to substitute their own. For any part of the session they may wish to allow more or less time than that suggested.

1 Introduce the theme   *3–6 minutes*

In what ways does successful interpersonal communication (dialogue, discussion, debate etc.) depend on cooperation?

2 Vocabulary   *3–6 minutes*

Can the children produce synonyms, antonyms and sentences for the difficult words (which were covered in the Circle Time session)?

3 The story   *6 minutes*

This could be told or read by the children.

4 Talking about the story   *10–20 minutes*

The teacher uses some of the questions and discussion points given, stimulating the children to talk about the story as a narrative. This helps the children to develop a (literary) meta-language.

5 The Literacy Time learning activity   *10–20 minutes*

These activities focus on oracy in group contexts. Some of the activities could be used in follow-up lessons.

| **Total time** | *30–60 minutes (approx.)* |

1 INTRODUCE THE THEME

Key points

- How does successful discussion require cooperation? (E.g. taking turns to speak, listening carefully to the points made by others.)

- What would be the advantages of writing with another person or persons? (E.g. bounce ideas off each other, pool experiences, two points of view/voices etc.)

2 VOCABULARY

Can you think of a word(s) that means the same as/the opposite to each of these? For each of the words, make up a sentence containing that word.

cascaded	flinch
squatting	sign
twirling	lip-read
flashing	kiln
disappeared	homesick
mystery	ornamental
isolated	

3 THE STORY:

With younger children – ask them to use their own words to tell the story (*The Mystery of the Missing Fish*) which they listened to in Circle Time. With older children, go round the class having the children (re-) read the story out loud. Alternatively, give the children time to (re-) read the story to themselves.

The Mystery of the Missing Fish

4 TALKING ABOUT THE STORY

Did the children understand?

- Why would Megan notice the frown on Mrs Cheshire's face?

- Why was Megan homesick?

- How do we know that Megan was a kind girl?

- Suggest three reasons why making a pottery heron was a good idea.

Points for discussion

- How do we know that Tyesha valued Megan's kindness in the storm?

- How can we tell that the three girls did not intend to be mean to Megan?

- Can you think of other cooperative projects which Megan could have suggested?

- What would it be like to be deaf? (Good things as well as negative ones.) E.g. feeling left out of conversations by hearing people; enjoying beautiful sights and scents even more; learning two languages – spoken and signing, etc.

- How can we be kind/helpful/cooperative towards deaf or hard-of-hearing people? (E.g. face them; learn sign language; don't mock; smile a greeting, etc.)

- What, for you, is the message of this story? (E.g. Communication is important. Cooperation is important. Having friends is important. Be understanding to each other. Being excluded, or homesick, is a painful experience.) The children should understand that there is not just one correct answer.

5 THE LEARNING ACTIVITY

1 **Songs and Poems** (resources needed: poetry or song anthologies)

In pairs or small groups, find a poem or song which connects with the story. (It could be about sight and sound, cooperation, fish and birds, storms, being home-sick, etc.) Ask some of the children to read out their chosen poem or song.

2 **Story discussion**

- Are there many stories about a deaf or disabled character? (Not many.) Does it matter? Can you think of how a disability (e.g. being blind or a wheelchair user) could give someone an advantage? How could this be used in a story?

- How do we learn about the world? (Through our five senses: sight, sound, smell, taste, touch.)

- Megan enjoyed the sights at the pond. (What were these?) What scents might she have noticed? (E.g. pondweeds, nearby flowers.) What sensations might she have felt? (E.g. breeze on her face.) If she was not deaf, what might she have heard? (E.g. plops in the water, the splashing of the fountain, bird calls, children or cars in the distance.)

3   Individual activity

- Imagine you are looking at a market stall. Describe the scene. Think about what you can see, smell, hear, touch, but write it as though you had one sense missing.

And/or

- Write a story with a disabled hero or heroine.

4   Group activity

- Working in pairs, write a story with a mystery.

- Perhaps your class could link up with a class from a special school. The two classes could cooperate on a common project. (You could use Circle Time to brainstorm for ideas about what this could be.)

The Mystery of the Missing Fish
Assembly
Theme: The value of Cooperation

Introduction
The assembly leader introduces the theme and talks about the benefits of cooperation and the importance of playing and working together. We often make friends through cooperation. Without friends we are lonely.

Story
Assembly leader:

Our story today is about how Megan thinks of a cooperative project and makes friends.

The assembly leader or a child reads the story – *The Mystery of the Missing Fish*

Poem or Song
You can choose a poem or a song, or both. Alternatively, you can have a child (or children) read the poems they chose or wrote in class and have one of the songs that were chosen. Select poems and songs which are relevant to the theme or which echo the story in some way.

Examples

Poem:

The Heron, by Gregory Harrison
Page 81 in *A Second Poetry Book*, published by Oxford University Press, 1980

Song:

Hands to Work and Feet to Run
No. 21 in *Someone's Singing Lord*, published by A&C Black, 2002.

Quiet reflection or prayer
For a universal, humanistic or multi-faith assembly:

Quiet reflection

The assembly leader says:
Think of how you feel if you have no one to play with. (Pause) Think of how we make friends. (Pause) Let us think of ways in which we can be good at cooperation today – in our work, in the playground, in Circle Time etc.

Or for Christian schools:

Prayer

Let us pray.

Dear God,

Comfort all those who feel lonely or isolated today. Help us to be friendly to others. Thank you for the gift of friendship. Help us to make friends and to be good friends and to develop our ability to cooperate with others.

Amen.

Chapter 7

Litter Lessons

Circle Time Seven

Teacher's Notes

Theme Seven: The value of **Protecting the Environment**

Circle Time Value: We need to value our environment. This means that we should protect it from harm (conserve it).

> Circle Time provides a forum in which the children can participate in reaching agreement about how to protect their own classroom environment.

Circle Time Plan

This five-part lesson plan is only a guide. Teachers are likely to add to or amend the learning activities which are suggested and may sometimes wish to substitute their own. For any part of the session they may wish to allow more or less time than that suggested.

1 Introduce the theme   *3–6 minutes*

We can **protect** our classroom **environment** from being spoiled by litter and other damage.

2 Vocabulary   *3–6 minutes*

The teacher ensures that the children understand the words given.

3 The story   *6 minutes*

The teacher shows the illustration and reads the story.

4 Talking about the story   *10–20 minutes*

The teacher uses some of the questions and discussion points given, stimulating the children to talk about the story/theme.

5 The Circle Time learning activity   *10–20 minutes*

These activities will help to improve or conserve a good classroom environment. Some suggested activities could be used in follow-up lessons.

Total time   *30–60 minutes (approx.)*

1 INTRODUCE THE THEME

Key points

- We can widen our circle of values by caring for the world outside of ourselves.

- We can care for the environment by protecting it from harm and by making improvements.

- Our immediate environment in school is the classroom.

- From what kind of damage can we protect our classroom? (E.g. Clutter. Litter. Noise. Dirt.)

---

2 VOCABULARY

Use your usual methods for introducing new words.

The difficult words in the story are:

chucked	–	threw
container	–	something to hold things in
crouching	–	bending low
plot	–	the story in sequence of events
fertiliser	–	enriching substance for soil
admired	–	looked up to
design	–	make a pattern
dumped	–	threw down
mess	–	untidy muddle
litter	–	untidy refuse; untidy rubbish
litter-lout	–	someone who leaves litter
scattered	–	sprinkled here and there; thrown in all directions
spoiled	–	ruined
septic	–	infected cut or wound
tilted	–	tipped to one side

3 THE STORY:

Litter Lessons

Litter Lessons

"Pick that up, Jack," Mum called. "This minute."

"Sorry," I said.

I was watering my patch of the garden and had chucked an empty plant-food container into the hedge. I picked it up and went to the bin by our gate. Shandy, my new sheepdog puppy, trotted after me. She's dead cute. She began to circle me, crouching every now and then as though I were a herd of sheep.

On the way back to the house I stopped for a final look at my plot. It was looking great. I'd been allowed to plant what I wanted so long as I looked after it. I'd dug into the bare ground, uncovering rich, dark soil beneath the hard crust. I'd chucked out stones and dug in fertiliser and grown thick, low flowers which completely covered the large square of bare soil in a pattern of green leaves and bright colours, framed by white blossom all round the edge.

"Hard work and imagination," Dad had said.

Shandy stood by my side and we admired it together. Everyone liked my design. It had been worth the hard work.

Back in the house Mum immediately asked me to go out to the bin again, with a black plastic bag of kitchen rubbish.

At the door I found my friend Kev, on his bike. He had been just about to knock.

"Coming for a ride?" he asked.

"Yeah, sure," I said. "I'll take this later." I dumped the black bag by the door, popped Shandy safely back inside the house and collected my bike from the shed. We had a great time, me and Kev, riding through the fields. We came across some dumped beer bottles and scored points for hitting them with a stone from quite a long way. It came out a draw. On the way home we rode down Bude Hill, no hands.

Luckily we reached home just before it poured with rain. Shandy came running to meet me, her tail wagging furiously. She was always dead pleased to see me. I bent down, pushing her about in a play-fight, which she loved.

At bedtime Shandy followed me up the stairs and when I settled down in bed with my Harry Potter book, she curled up beside me. It was cosy until Mum came up to switch off the light.

"Just look at this mess," she said, frowning at my room. My clothes and things littered the floor.

"You can pick all this up tomorrow, Jack. You're turning into a real litter-lout. And Shandy can't sleep there either." She kissed me goodnight and carried Shandy downstairs.

I listened to the rain rattling hard on my window. I liked the drumming sound, and when I drifted off to sleep I dreamed that I was drumming on a big, black, plastic drum and the clothes on my bedroom floor rose into the air and, like big cloth birds, they flapped round the room before flying out of the window.

The dream was so vivid that I was almost surprised to find my clothes were still there in the morning, though when I began to get dressed, I discovered that my T-shirt was missing. It was my favourite. My Man United. Could it really have blown out of the window? I parted the curtains and looked out. I had a shock. The garden was littered with rubbish: soggy newspaper, packages, tins and cartons were strewn everywhere, including on my patch. I pulled on an ordinary T-shirt and ran downstairs to the garden. I saw immediately that Shandy had chewed a hole in the black bag which I'd left by the door. She'd scattered the rubbish everywhere. She'd trampled some of the plants in my flower design, playing with the rubbish.

"You bad pup," I said crossly, dismayed by my ruined garden. She hung her head.

"Don't blame Shandy," Mum called from the door. "You left the bag there, and you can pick it all up before breakfast."

Shandy stayed with me and licked my hand as I collected up the rubbish. I was still cross with her and pushed her away.

After it was done I was ravenous, but as I bolted down my cornflakes I noticed something screwed up in a corner near Shandy's bed. I picked it up. It was my lost T-shirt, well chewed and even more spoiled than my garden.

"Oh Shandy!" I said, sadly.

She gave a small, uncertain shake of her tail.

"Puppies chew," said Mum. "You mustn't leave your clothes on the floor."

There and then I was made to go and tidy my room. What a rotten day it was turning out to be. It got even worse. When we took Shandy up to the field for her walk she yelped as she was running, and then limped over to us. Mum picked her up, turning over her paw. A piece of glass was stuck there. She was bleeding badly.

"Some idiot has left a broken bottle," Mum said.

I didn't dare confess that it may have been me.

In the vet's waiting room, poor Shandy was shaking with fear. I stroked her, telling her softly that it would be soon be better. I was sorry I'd been mad at her and so sorry that I had left that broken glass. I hated having to hold her while the vet pulled it out.

"She'll be OK as long as it doesn't go septic," he said.

Every night that week, as gently as I could, I bathed Shandy's paw. She watched, her head tilted to one side. She knew I was trying to help. After a few days, she was running about again – back to her same old self. I had changed though. I had learned a lesson that I would never forget.

4 TALKING ABOUT THE STORY

Did the children understand?

- Why did Dad say that Jack had used imagination on his plot?

- Why was the spoiled garden Jack's own fault?

- Why might the broken glass have been Jack's fault too?

- What was the lesson Jack had learned?

Points for discussion

- In what ways can litter be dangerous? (E.g. cutting children or creatures, litter flapping onto cars, plastic bags to young children.)

- In what other ways, besides litter, can we spoil our classroom environment? (E.g. clutter and untidiness; noise pollution; damage; dirt.)

- Why is protecting and improving the environment important? (Less dangerous, more enjoyable; life enhancing; cheers us up, etc.)

5 THE CIRCLE TIME LEARNING ACTIVITY

1 Warm-up game

The children trot round the outside of the circle like cloth birds, pretending to flap their cloth wings. When the teacher says **Search**, they flap round the classroom spying out litter on the floor, and picking it up if they see any. They return to their Circle Time chairs when the teacher claps his or her hands. Going round the circle, in turn, the children place any litter they found into a bin in the centre of the circle. The other children clap.

2 Circle contribution

Go round the circle for suggestions about how to keep the classroom a safe and pleasant place to be.

3 Circle discussion

Lead the children into a discussion of what classroom rules they would like to have.

(i) About litter

(ii) About noise (sound litter!)

(iii) About keeping things in the right place

What happens if some people do not keep these rules? Does anyone have a problem with keeping one of these rules? Could we help him/her to keep that rule?

Take the opportunity for a widening discussion of environmental issues – from classroom, school and playground, to home, neighbourhood and world.

4   Circle group work

Go round the circle for rule suggestions. Briefly discuss each suggestion and, if there is agreement on a rule, add it to a **Rule Chart for Classroom Environment** (page 105). The chart can then be pinned on the classroom wall.

Rule Chart for Classroom Environment

- Talk quietly

- Put litter in the bin

- Pick up litter that you notice

etc.

Litter Lessons

Literacy Hour Seven

Teacher's Notes

Theme Seven: The value of protecting the **Environment**

Literacy Skills: Using a story to endorse a moral rule or principle.

| Literacy Hour provides a regular time in which to explore the ways in which values are inherent in stories.

Literacy Hour Plan

This five-part lesson plan is only a guide. Teachers are likely to add to or amend the learning activities which are suggested and may sometimes wish to substitute their own. For any part of the session they may wish to allow more or less time than that suggested.

1 Introduce the theme *3–6 minutes*

How do stories embody and reveal values?

2 Vocabulary *3–6 minutes*

Can the children produce synonyms, antonyms and sentences for the difficult words (which were covered in the Circle Time session)?

3 The story *6 minutes*

This could be told or read by the children.

4 Talking about the story *10–20 minutes*

The teacher uses some of the questions and discussion points given, stimulating the children to talk about the story as a narrative. This helps the children to develop a (literary) meta-language.

5 The Literacy Time learning activity *10–20 minutes*

These "literacy activities" focus on the environment as their theme. Some of the activities could be used in follow-up lessons.

Total time *30–60 minutes (approx.)*

1 INTRODUCE THE THEME

Key points

- We all share a responsibility for keeping our classroom pleasant and tidy.

- We need rules to help us to do this. (Give and ask for examples, e.g. don't drop litter.)

2 VOCABULARY

Can you think of a word(s) that means the same as/the opposite to each of these? For each of the words, make up a sentence containing that word.

patched	litter
chucked	litter-lout
dumped	spoiled
mess	fertiliser

3 THE STORY:

With younger children – ask them to use their own words to tell the story (*Litter Lessons*) which they listened to in Circle Time. With older children, go round the class having the children (re-) read the story out loud. Alternatively, give the children time to (re-) read the story to themselves.

Litter Lessons

4 TALKING ABOUT THE STORY

Did the children understand?

- How do we know that Jack was cross with Shandy?

- How does Jack try to calm Shandy's fear at the vets?

Points for discussion

- Jack learns a definite and direct lesson in this story. Do not cause litter; it can be dangerous. Do stories always have a direct lesson? How could there be an indirect lesson? (E.g. something you learn rather than the character does. A value implicit in the story – not explicitly stated.)

- What are the lesson/message/values in:

  Cinderella (e.g. don't be mean to people)
  Little Red Riding Hood (e.g. don't talk to strangers)

- Could a story have no values/messages whatsoever?

- What, for you, is the message of this story? We know there is a direct message in this story – against litter. Is there an indirect message? What do you think it could be? (E.g. With hard work and imagination you can make a beautiful garden. Dreams are powerful. Mums often try to improve our behaviour. We can really love our pets.) The children should understand that there is not just one correct answer.

5 THE LEARNING ACTIVITY

1 **Songs and Poems** (resources needed: poetry or song anthologies)

   In pairs or small groups, find a poem or song which connects with the story. (It could be about litter, pets, gardening, etc.)

2 **Story discussion**

   Let the children talk about stories they like (in books, films, television) and the values/messages which they promote. Try to show the children that all stories have values/messages, that good ones often have several and work on several levels, and that on the whole, in good stories, the values/messages are indirect – rather than obvious or preachy.

3 **Individual activity**

   - Let the children write a story with a moral message, trying not to "preach" (be didactic).
   - Read the following poem:

Lousy, Loathsome Litter

A spreading stench
Of paper rags
With broken glass
From torn black bags.

A festering mass
Of messy wraps
And smelly scraps
And jagged tins
From spilling bins.

Worms and germs,
A fat, rat's tat.
Lousy, Loathsome Litter

Talk about it. The children could write a poem with the same title: Lousy, Loathsome Litter.

4   Group activity

Divide the children into groups of four. Give each group a small selection of books. (E.g. one picture book; one narrative poem or song; one of the other short stories from this book; a short novel/story that has been read by the class.) Each group must explore each book in their pile, and together analyse the values, messages, moral rules or lessons to be found in pictures, events, dialogue, characters, etc. The groups could feed back their findings to the whole class.

Litter Lessons
Assembly
Theme: Protecting the Environment

Introduction
The assembly leader introduces the theme and talks about why we should look after the environment. Give examples of this in school, in town and in the countryside.

Story
Assembly leader

Our story today is about Jack. Thanks to his puppy, Shandy, Jack learns a litter-lesson he will never forget.

The assembly leader or a child reads the story – *Litter Lessons*.

Poem or Song
You can choose a poem or a song, or both. Alternatively, you can have a child (or children) read the poems they chose or wrote in class and have one of the songs that were chosen. Select poems and songs which are relevant to the theme or which echo the story in some way.

Examples

Poems:

The Boy who Dropped Litter, by Lindsay MacRae
In *The Poetry Book*, published by Dolphin, 1996.

The Dustbin Men, by Gregory Harrison
In *A First Poetry Book*, published by Oxford University Press, 1979.

Song:

Milk Bottle Tops and Paper Bags
No. 17 in *Someone's Singing Lord*, published by A&C Black, 2002

Quiet reflection or prayer
For a universal, humanistic or multi-faith assembly:

Quiet reflection

The assembly leader says:
Picture a neat, pleasant classroom in your mind. (Pause) Now picture an untidy, unpleasant classroom. (Pause) Think about how you feel in pleasant surroundings compared to unpleasant ones. (Pause) Think of one thing that you could do to make your classroom more attractive.

Or for Christian schools:

Prayer

Let us pray.

Lord,

Thank you for our beautiful world – the grass, trees, flowers, the countryside, seaside, cities and villages. Fill our hearts with gratitude and respect for your creation so that we will guard it from damage and litter. Show us how to look after your world. Help us to keep our class-rooms and our school as pleasant and safe as we can and to look after plants and flowers and all of your creatures.

Amen.

Chapter 8

Wish Upon a Rainbow

Circle Time Eight

Teacher's Notes

Theme Eight: The value of our **Appreciation of the natural world**

Circle Time Value: Appreciation in the classroom.

Circle Time provides a forum in which children can consider how to enhance their surroundings and develop their aesthetic appreciation of their visual environment.

Circle Time Plan

This five-part lesson plan is only a guide. Teachers are likely to add to or amend the learning activities which are suggested and may sometimes wish to substitute their own. For any part of the session they may wish to allow more or less time than that suggested.

1 Introduce the theme *3–6 minutes*

We can enhance our classroom environment with good artwork, plants and other beautiful and natural objects.

2 Vocabulary *3–6 minutes*

The teacher ensures that the children understand the words given.

3 The story *6 minutes*

The teacher shows the illustration and reads the story.

4 Talking about the story *10–20 minutes*

The teacher uses some of the questions and discussion points given, stimulating the children to talk about the story/theme.

5 The Circle Time learning activity *10–20 minutes*

These activities seek to develop the children's appreciation. Some suggested activities could be used in follow-up lessons.

| Total time | *30–60 minutes (approx.)* |

1 INTRODUCE THE THEME

Key points

- We can appreciate our environment – from the small things that make a pleasant classroom to the wonderful things in nature, like colour and rainbows.

- Not only can we seek to protect the environment, we can enhance and improve it.

- What kind of things can we do to improve our classroom? (E.g. display interesting and beautiful work and pictures.)

2 VOCABULARY

Use your usual methods for introducing new words.

The difficult words in the story are:

arched	–	curved
oblivious	–	unaware
adventure	–	bold, risky exploit or event
knight	–	a rank from medieval order or chivalry
shimmered	–	shone with quivering light
forbidden	–	not allowed
tangles	–	knotted
tendrils	–	hanging vegetation
urging	–	encouraging
plunged	–	jumped into; dived into
gloom	–	dark shade
gobble	–	eat up quickly
wonder	–	amazement
drab	–	colourless

3 THE STORY:

Wish Upon a Rainbow

Wish Upon a Rainbow

The sky was blue and the sun was yellow, but to Aidan the world seemed grey. He hated school and school was starting up again tomorrow. Suddenly it began to rain – big, fat splodges like tears from above. Aidan raised his face to the cooling drops and saw the rainbow. It arched across the sky like a brightly painted bridge. Aidan gazed at it, oblivious to the rain.

"Aidan, come inside," called his Mum.

Aidan went indoors, and he and Mum looked out through the window.

"I can see red, orange, yellow, green, blue and purple," Aidan said. "Dark and light purple, right, Mum?"

"The dark purple is a deep colour called indigo and the light purple is called violet," said Mum. "The colours spell 'ROYGBIV'. It will melt when the rain stops. Grandma always said we could have three wishes while it's still there."

"Can I?" said Aidan.

"Of course," said Mum.

"I wish I didn't have to go to school," Aidan said, immediately.

"Well you can't get that," said Mum. "But perhaps you'll get to like it better."

"Maybe win a prize for parents' day," said Aidan. "Like Sam." Sam was Aidan's best friend.

"That's only two wishes," Mum said.

Aidan closed his eyes to think. He must make his third wish before the rainbow melted away.

"I wish I could have an adventure," he decided.

That night Aidan had a vivid dream. He dreamt that he was a knight of old on a white horse. He set out to find an adventure. After galloping for many miles he came to a wide river. A huge waterfall towered about him. Hundreds of tiny rainbows shimmered, almost danced in the spray. Aidan saw a dark space behind the waterfall and cautiously rode his horse along the narrow ledge. Bravely he rode the entire length of the ledge, and in a cave near the other side he found the Rainbow Man. Aidan recognised the Rainbow Man from his red hair, orange hat, bright green eyes, yellow jacket, blue shoes, indigo trousers and violet shirt.

"If you want an adventure," said the Rainbow Man, "you must enter the Forbidden Forest." Aidan discovered the forest to be very dark with densely growing trees and tangles of tendrils hanging down from their branches. He took a deep breath and, urging his horse, plunged into the gloom. There were no colours in the forest. Everything was shadowed and dark. With difficulty, he travelled some way in, when a net descended over him, like a trap. Beyond the net he could make out a tall woman with the fierce eyes of a tiger.

"Give the right password and I'll let you go," said the Tiger Woman. "Otherwise I'll gobble you up."

Aidan was frightened. He thought very hard.

"ROYGBIV," he said at last, and suddenly he was whirled off his horse and through the air, coming to rest at Rainbow's End where he found seven gold pots. Each held paint of a different colour – deep, rich colours – Red, Orange, Yellow, Green, Blue, Indigo and Violet.

"These are the paints that have painted the Universe," said a voice. "The birds and butterflies, the dragonflies and dandelions, the ladybirds and lilies, the flowers and tropical fish. Because they are magic pots, they will never run dry."

At that point, Aidan woke up and remembered his dream. *I'm glad I dream in colour*, he thought.

At breakfast he told his dream to his Mum.

"That was like having an adventure," she said. "There's one wish already!"

"Well, I still wish I didn't have to go to school," Aidan said. "It's so boring, Mum, can't you send a note?"

"No," said Mum. "You're not ill, Aidan. You've got to go."

That day Aidan had a new teacher. Aidan was surprised when he first saw him. Mr Rogers had red hair, green eyes and a purple shirt.

"He doesn't look a bit like a teacher," whispered Sam.

He looks just like the Rainbow Man, Aidan thought.

That afternoon they had an Art lesson.

"I want you all to paint something that shows the wonder of the world," said Mr Rogers.

Aidan painted a rainbow. He painted drab brown birds and fishes flying into the rainbow, and flying out again glowing with rainbow colours. He called his picture, "The Wonder of Colour", and Mr Rogers liked it very much. He showed Aidan how to mix colours to make new ones, and Aidan was surprised when it was home time already. He realised that he'd enjoyed the afternoon. In fact, with Mr Rogers as his teacher, he began to like going to school.

At the end of term, Aidan won the Art Prize for his rainbow picture and he remembered his three wishes.

"In a way they all came true, right, Mum?" he said.

4 TALKING ABOUT THE STORY

Did the children understand?

- What were Aiden's three wishes?

- Why was "The Wonder of Colour" a good title for Aiden's rainbow picture?

Points for discussion

- How can we use colour to make the classroom more beautiful?

- Does colour make the world more beautiful?

- What other things in the natural world are "wonderful"? (E.g. creatures, birds, flowers, waves on the sea, etc.)

5 THE CIRCLE TIME LEARNING ACTIVITY

1 **Warm-up game**

The children take turns to be in the centre of the circle. They must make a wish. They give a clue(s) to their wish and the seated children guess what the wish is. (Children may make the same wish as a previous child, but must give a different clue.)

2 **Circle contribution**

Go round the circle asking children their favourite colour. Why do they like it? Go round the circle for suggestions about how we can improve/enhance the classroom environment. Good suggestions could subsequently be acted upon (e.g. bringing in plants for a plant corner, natural objects for a nature table.)

3 **Circle discussion**

(i) What do we appreciate about our classroom? About the wider world?

(ii) The rainbow and its colours gave Aiden a sense of wonder. What other "wonderful" things exist in "nature"?

4 **Circle group work**

(i) Paint a rainbow on a big sheet of paper. Pin this on the wall. Write "The Wonder of Colour" at the top. Each child should do two small drawings/paintings of the same natural object; one in greys only and one glowing with colour. The children should select something colourful which they like – e.g. a peacock, a rose, a ladybird, a shell, etc. The children could paste their drawings – the grey picture on the outside and all the colourful pictures on the inside of the rainbow.

(ii) *What Happened Next?*
The children are going to make up their own Circle Time "Dream Adventure" with wonderful sights and daring deeds. Begin by saying:

One night Aiden had a vivid dream. He set out to find an adventure. He walked for many miles until he came to a huge palace. The drawbridge was down and the gates open. Aiden was thirsty. He went in to ask for a glass of water – *what happened next?*

Go round the circle. Each child adds to the story and then passes it on.

Wish Upon a Rainbow

Literacy Hour Eight

Teacher's Notes

Theme Eight: The value of **Appreciation of the Environment**

Literacy Skills: The power of the visual environment is used to stimulate creative writing.

| **Literacy Hour provides a regular time to develop a creative response (in poems and descriptive prose) to the beautiful and wonderful natural world.**

Literacy Hour Plan

This five-part lesson plan is only a guide. Teachers are likely to add to or amend the learning activities which are suggested and may sometimes wish to substitute their own. For any part of the session they may wish to allow more or less time than that suggested.

1 Introduce the theme   *3–6 minutes*

How can we use the natural world in our writing?

2 Vocabulary   *3 6 minutes*

Can the children produce synonyms, antonyms and sentences for the difficult words (which were covered in the Circle Time session)?

3 The story   *6 minutes*

This could be told or read by the children.

4 Talking about the story   *10–20 minutes*

The teacher uses some of the questions and discussion points given, stimulating the children to talk about the story as a narrative. This helps the children to develop a (literary) meta-language.

5 The Literacy Time learning activity   *10–20 minutes*

Some of the suggested "literacy" activities encourage group work as a positive enhancement of the Circle Time skills and values. Some of the activities could be used in follow-up lessons.

Total time | *30–60 minutes (approx.)*

1 INTRODUCE THE THEME

Key points

- The beauty and wonder of the natural world has stimulated writers since the beginnings of literacy.

- We can use our senses (what would you see, hear, smell, feel?) when we describe a beautiful place.

2 VOCABULARY

Can you think of a word(s) that means the same as/the opposite to each of these? For each of the words, make up a sentence containing that word.

arched	adventure
oblivious	knight
forbidden	shimmered
tangles	tendrils
gloom	urging
gobble	plunged
drab	wonder

3 THE STORY:

With younger children – ask them to use their own words to tell the story (*Wish Upon a Rainbow*) which they listened to in Circle Time. With older children, go round the class having the children (re-) read the story out loud. Alternatively, give the children time to (re-) read the story to themselves.

Wish Upon a Rainbow

4 TALKING ABOUT THE STORY

Did the children understand?

- Why did the forest seem to have no colour?

- How was the Tiger Woman like a tiger?

- Why did Aiden think that Mr Rogers looked like the Rainbow Man?

Points for discussion

- Why did the world seem "grey" at the end of Aiden's holiday?

- Why was Aiden's dream like having an adventure?

- Can you think of other stories about having a wish or wishes?

- What, for you, is the message of this story? (E.g. Wishes can come true. The world is a wonderful place. We can use our wonder/appreciation of the world in our creative work.) The children should understand that there is not just one correct answer.

5 THE LEARNING ACTIVITY

1   **Songs and Poems** (resources needed: poetry or song anthologies)

In pairs or small groups, find a poem or song which connects with the story. (It could be about wishes, adventures, colour.) Ask some of the children to read out their chosen poem or song.

2   **Story discussion**

Discuss some of the ways in which colour is used in the story. Ask: What colours would you use in a sad story? What colours would you use in a happy story? What colours would you use in a violent story? What colours would you use in a peaceful story?

3   **Individual activity**

(i)   Write a description of a sad person. Think of their face, hair, age, manner, voice, etc. And, of course, describe their clothes. Remember to use some "sad" colours.

(ii) Now write a description of a happy person.

(iii) Imagine that your sad and happy characters are talking to each other, about what they like in nature. Write down their conversation.

(iv) Read some good nature poems to the children. They can then write their own nature poem.

4   Group activity

Your own adventure

Collectively the children make up an adventure story in the **first** person. In a group they decide on answers to these questions:

The Beginning

Where did I go? (Choose a beautiful place)
Why did I go there?
Who went with me?

The Middle

What happened?
How did I feel?
What happened next?
What did I do?

The End

What happened at the end?

Next, suggest a beautiful place not chosen by the group (e.g. the seaside). The children decide on their own individual answers to these questions to make their own story. They practise telling their completed story to a partner. Finally some (all?) of the children tell their stories to the whole class.

Wish Upon a Rainbow

Assembly

Theme: Appreciation of the Natural World

Introduction

The assembly leader introduces the theme and talks about how we live in a beautiful world of lakes, forests, oceans, mountains, trees, flowers, animals, birds and fishes. There are many wonderful creations – think of the stars, of waves on the sea, of rainbows, of dolphins, peacocks, seahorses and seashells. If we experience the wonder of the natural world we will add joy to our lives and care about protecting our earth.

Story

Assembly leader:

Our story today is about Aiden, who loves the glowing colours of the rainbow. He makes three wishes, hoping that the magical rainbow will help them to come true.

The assembly leader or a child reads the story – *Wish Upon a Rainbow*.

Poem or Song

You can choose a poem or a song, or both. Alternatively, you can have a child (or children) read the poems they chose or wrote in class and have one of the songs that were chosen. Select poems and songs which are relevant to the theme or which echo the story in some way.

Examples

Poem:

What is Red? by Mary O'Neill
In *A First Poetry Book*, published by Oxford University Press, 1979.

Song:

The World is Such a Lovely Place
No. 8 in *Every Colour Under the Sun*, published by Ward Lock Educational Co. Ltd, 1983.

Quiet reflection or prayer

For a universal, humanistic or multi-faith assembly:

Quiet reflection

The assembly leader says:
Think of some of the beautiful things on the earth. (Pause) Think of something that fills you with wonder. (Pause) Let us feel thankful for our wonderful world.

Or for Christian schools:

Prayer

Let us pray.

God, the Creator,
Fill our hearts with gratitude and wonder at the beautiful world you have created for us. Give us the desire and the wisdom to look after this earth, our home.

Amen.

Chapter 9

Circle of Trees

Circle Time Nine

Teacher's Notes

Theme Nine: The value of Circle Time **Democracy**

Circle Time Value: Children can come to appreciate the democratic approach which underpins Circle Time.

> Circle Time provides a forum in which we can practice democratic participation and decision-making.

Circle Time Plan

This five-part lesson plan is only a guide. Teachers are likely to add to or amend the learning activities which are suggested and may sometimes wish to substitute their own. For any part of the session they may wish to allow more or less time than that suggested.

1 Introduce the theme   *3–6 minutes*

What is **democracy**? How is Circle Time democratic?

2 Vocabulary   *3–6 minutes*

The teacher ensures that the children understand the words given.

3 The story   *6 minutes*

The teacher shows the illustration and reads the story.

4 Talking about the story   *10–20 minutes*

The teacher uses some of the questions and discussion points given, stimulating the children to talk about the story/theme.

5 The Circle Time learning activity   *10–20 minutes*

This story and the activities connects, directly, with Circle Time values. Some suggested activities could be used in follow-up lessons.

Total time *30–60 minutes (approx.)*

1 INTRODUCE THE THEME

Key points

- What is democracy?

- Why is it valuable? (E.g. Avoids conflict. Promotes fairness.)

- What are democratic values? (Equality, justice, freedom.)

- How is Circle Time democratic?

- Can we make our Circle Time more democratic?

2 VOCABULARY

Use your usual methods for introducing new words.

The difficult words in the story are:

glared	–	stared fiercely
expectantly	–	waiting with anticipation
bicker	–	argue
thief	–	one who steals
dappled	–	speckled
canopy	–	overhanging shelter
weathered	–	affected or aged by weather
dents	–	hollows or marks left by blows or pressure
enchanted	–	magical
glade	–	clear grassy space in a wood or forest
vote	–	make your formal, rightful choice
lingered	–	delayed, loitered, remained a long time

3 THE STORY:

Circle of Trees

Circle of Trees

Lauren had no one to play with at home, but here, at Aunty Betty's new house, she had her twin cousins, Sarah and Jane, and she was staying for two whole weeks.

"Now girls," said Aunty Betty at breakfast on the first day of Lauren's visit. "Each afternoon I'll take you out. Where should we go today, d'you think?"

"Swimming," said Sarah immediately.

"No. On the boat at the park," said Jane.

"I picked first!" Sarah said. She smiled at Lauren.

"I bet you like swimming, Lauren, don't you?"

Jane glared at her twin.

"But Lauren's never been on the boat," she said.

Both girls looked at her expectantly.

"I really don't mind," Lauren said.

"But we always go to the boring old park," said Sarah.

"But not on the boat," said Jane. "That's the point, silly."

"Be quiet, you two," said Aunty Betty. "You do nothing but bicker. We won't go anywhere if you're not careful, so don't spoil things for Lauren."

The twins did shut up, but they continued to glare at each other over the table.

After breakfast Aunty Betty went off to her workroom.

"What shall we play?" said Lauren.

Jane was pulling off her navy-blue cardy. She wore a buttercup yellow T-shirt underneath.

"That's mine, you thief," Sarah yelled.

"Liar," shouted Jane.

"T'is!"

"T'isn't!"

"T'is." Sarah tugged at the yellow T-shirt and Jane twisted away. There was a tearing sound.

"Now look what you've made me do," said Sarah.

"To *my* T-shirt!" said Jane.

She pulled her sister's hair in fury and Sarah kicked out at her, trying to make her let go.

"Stop. Please, please," said Lauren.

Her cousins rounded on her.

"How would you like your best T-shirt to be ripped?" Jane demanded.

"She started it," hissed Sarah.

Lauren put her hands over her ears.

"Anyway, mind your own business," Sarah said, pulling Lauren's hands away so that she would hear.

"Please, please," added Jane, mimicking Lauren's voice.

That was it! Lauren fled out into the garden and strode away from the house, walking off her anger and agitation. By the time she reached the orchard at the end of Aunty Betty's garden, all she felt was bitter disappointment. Her dreams of a happy time with her cousins had been smashed.

Lauren squeezed between two closely growing trees. Her eyes widened at what she saw and a feeling of wonder melted all her disappointment away.

She found herself in a dappled, green clearing, a perfect grass circle ringed by closely growing trees. The trees reached out above, almost touching, creating a natural den. Sunshine slanted through this leafy canopy, lighting up leaves of crimson and gold and making moving patterns on the grass below. Lauren gazed at all this before she noticed three flat stones set into the ground.

She sat down on one of these, leaning back against the tree behind, and closed her eyes. Lauren breathed deeply, breathing in the clean, calm air. When she opened her eyes again the sun was shining, like a spotlight, through the open centre of the canopy of leaves, directly over a piece of wood on the ground. The wood had been weathered into the shape of a bird – head, neck and folded wings. Lauren picked up the wood and stroked the smooth curves. She noticed that even the small dents on each side of the rounded head looked just like the dark eyes of a bird. The object was as beautiful as the magical place where it lived.

Lauren wondered if her cousins would like it here, would feel the peacefulness of the place, and this gave her an idea. After a last admiring gaze at the glowing colours of the leaves she replaced the wooden bird and ran back to fetch the others.

"It's lovely," said Aunty Betty. "The trees have formed an enchanted glade!"

"I love the autumn colours," said Sarah.

"I love the way the tree branches almost make a roof," said Jane, gazing up.

"I was thinking," said Lauren. "It reminds me of Circle Time at school. Why don't we come here every morning. Just us kids. Look, three stones. One each to sit on. We can decide where to go in the afternoon, and solve any problems or quarrels."

Everyone began to speak at once. Lauren bent and picked up the bird-shaped piece of wood.

"Look," she said.

Everyone stopped talking, curious to see what she had found.

"You can only speak if you are holding this Dove of Peace," she said. Sit on a stone, everyone, and put up your hand for the Dove.

Sarah was the first. She plonked down on the nearest stone and shot up her hand. Lauren handed her the Dove.

"It's a great idea," she said. "I wish we had Circle Time at our school. You go in now Mum. We must have our first meeting."

Aunty Betty smiled and went back to the house. Jane put up her hand and Sarah gave her the Dove.

"We should all make a choice about where we go this afternoon. We can give a reason if we want. Then we'll take a vote."

Lauren and Sarah nodded.

"I vote for the boat," Jane continued. "We don't usually go on the boat when we go to the park. Mum will let us while Lauren is here."

Lauren had the Dove next.

"It's sunny today. It might rain tomorrow. So I'll vote for the boat too. I'll be happy to vote for the swimming tomorrow."

"OK," said Sarah, taking the Dove. "I'll vote for the swimming tomorrow too. Today we'll go on the boat."

All that fortnight Lauren was amazed at how well the Circle of Trees seemed to work. Every morning they took their stone seats. They even went in the rain and the canopy above kept their den almost dry. It was so peaceful there, *like a powerful magic*, Lauren thought, that they never quarreled. They made their decision about the afternoon outing and even settled other things too. This helped to stop any quarrels outside the den.

"Let's discuss it in our Circle of Trees," one of them would say. All three girls kept to the rule about the Dove.

On the final morning, Lauren lingered behind after the twins had gone back to the house.

"Thank you," she whispered to the Dove and the trees.

For one last time she gazed at the patterns and colours, enjoyed the peace as she stroked the smooth head of the wooden bird. She thought about asking if she could take it home with her. *But no*, she thought. *It belongs here*. Gently Lauren placed the Dove back in the centre of the circle and ran to the house, ready to welcome her Dad, who was coming to take her back home.

4 TALKING ABOUT THE STORY

Did the children understand?

- Why had Lauren looked forward to this holiday at Aunty Betty's?

- Why did the natural den remind Lauren of Circle Time at school?

- Why did Lauren vote for the boat on the first day?

- How did the den settle quarrels that took place elsewhere?

- Why did Lauren leave the Dove in the den when she went home?

Points for discussion

- Why is it good to have some kind of Dove (a turn-to-speak token, or a rule) at Circle Time?

- When/why is it good to take a vote in Circle Time?

- What disagreements could we discuss and settle in our Circle Time?

5 THE CIRCLE TIME LEARNING ACTIVITY

1 Warm-up game

Talk about why people sometimes quarrel. Ask the children how Lauren would have felt if her Circle of Trees had not worked (i.e. her cousins continued to quarrel all of the holiday). Go round the circle with "I think Lauren would feel ____" Write the words suggested by the children (e.g. disappointed, sad, angry, fed up, cross). Now read the list. Each child should mime (with their face) the word they gave. Finally, say the words again. Any children who said the same word should change places – to be in a different chair (however many children said that word they should all change to a different chair).

2 Circle contribution

Go round the circle asking the children what activity they would choose to do if there was a free-choice session that afternoon or later in the week (e.g. painting, library, dancing, football, swimming). Note these. Delete those that are not possible (e.g. swimming may not be possible that afternoon). Vote on those remaining. The activity that receives the most votes is Activity One. The children who did not vote for Activity One vote for one of the remaining activities. The activity that receives the most votes is Activity Two. Repeat this process for one or two more activities. On the "free" afternoon, set up the three or four elected activities. The children opt into the one they prefer (e.g. painting or reading or football). (If only one member of staff is available, you may have to divide the session into two, to accommodate the first two choices).

3   Circle discussion

- Take any disagreements mentioned in the discussion following the story and use these as the focus for the Circle Time discussion.

- This is an opportunity to discuss your own Circle Time: its approach, activities, aims and rules. Do the children like it? What would they change?

4   Circle group work

(i)   This is also an opportunity for the group to decide (extend, review, confirm or change) the Circle Time rules. Make a chart of those upon which the group agrees. Or:

(ii) Ask the children what would happen if there were no rules (e.g. keeping to the left on the road; taking turns to talk at Circle Time). Ask each child to say what they think is the most important rule we have (in the classroom and/or in Circle Time). NB. Children could put these in order of importance on the Classroom and/or Circle Time rules chart.

Circle Time Rules

(1)   Only speak when you have the token.

(2)   In Circle Time we can discuss the actions of people but not say their names.

(3)   . . . .

Circle of Trees

Literacy Hour Nine

Teacher's Notes

Theme Nine: The value of **Democracy** in the classroom

Literacy Skills: Understanding democratic processes and values in group work.

> Literacy Hour provides a regular time in which appropriate group work encourages democratic practices in group literacy projects. It also provides an opportunity to use literacy skills in the service of democracy.

Literacy Hour Plan

This five-part lesson plan is only a guide. Teachers are likely to add to or amend the learning activities which are suggested and may sometimes wish to substitute their own. For any part of the session they may wish to allow more or less time than that suggested.

1 Introduce the theme
3–6 minutes

How can we use our literacy skills as democratic citizens? (E.g. write to our MP.)

2 Vocabulary
3–6 minutes

Can the children produce synonyms, antonyms and sentences for the difficult words (which were covered in the Circle Time session)?

3 The story
6 minutes

This could be told or read by the children.

4 Talking about the story
10–20 minutes

The teacher uses some of the questions and discussion points given, stimulating the children to talk about the story as a narrative. This helps the children to develop a (literary) meta-language.

5 The Literacy Time learning activity
10–20 minutes

Some of the suggested "literacy" activities encourage group work as a positive enhancement of the Circle Time skills and values. Some of the activities could be used in follow-up lessons.

Total time *30–60 minutes (approx.)*

1 INTRODUCE THE THEME

Key points

- Why is literacy useful in a democracy?

- How can we help ourselves to become more literate?

- How can a teacher help pupils to become literate?

2 VOCABULARY

Can you think of a word(s) that means the same as/the opposite to each of these? For each of the words, make up a sentence containing that word.

expectantly	glared
bicker	canopy
thief	glade
dappled	vote
dents	weathered
lingered	enchanted

3 THE STORY:

With younger children – ask them to use their own words to tell the story (*Circle of Trees*) which they listened to in Circle Time. With older children, go round the class having the children (re-) read the story out loud. Alternatively, give the children time to (re-) read the story to themselves.

Circle of Trees

4 TALKING ABOUT THE STORY

Did the children understand?

- How did the Circle of Trees save Lauren's holiday from being spoiled?

- Where would you say that this story divides into Beginning, Middle, End?

Points for discussion

- What are the advantages of taking a vote to make a collective decision?

- Could there be any disadvantages to this system?

- What, for you, is the message of this story? (E.g. Rows spoil things. Peaceful places make you feel calm. Democracy is good.)

5 THE LEARNING ACTIVITY

1 **Songs and Poems** (resources needed: poetry or song anthologies)

In pairs or small groups, find a poem or song which connects with the story. (It could be about circles, trees, birds, democracy, peace, quarrels, etc.) Ask some of the children to read out their chosen poem or song.

2 **Story discussion**

- What do you like about this story?

- What do you dislike about it?

- What kind of person is Lauren?

3 **Individual activity**

Let the children watch the television news (or remind them of items which have been in the news recently) and they can select something which they would like to express their views about. They could write to their MP (if you have names and address of local MP(s) these could actually be posted).

And/or the children could write a letter to the Head teacher about an issue within school.

4 **Group activity**

Note down the subjects which the children wrote about in their letters. Vote to select a subject for debate. Conduct a formal debate with proposer and seconder on each side, discussion points, and a vote after the summing-up.

Circle of Trees

Assembly

Theme: Democracy and Democratic Values

Introduction

The assembly leader introduces the theme and talks about how democracy is based on equal rights for everyone – for example, every adult citizen having the vote about who should be in government; or every member of the class having a vote about something that will affect the whole class. This is fair. He or she talks about why it is bad for all the power to be with just one person (a dictatorship).

Story

Assembly leader

Our story today is about a young girl whose holiday was saved when she introduced a democratic way to solve family squabbles.

The assembly leader or a child reads the story – *Circle of Trees*.

Poem or Song

You can choose a poem or a song, or both. Alternatively, you can have a child (or children) read the poems they chose or wrote in class and have one of the songs that were chosen. Select poems and songs which are relevant to the theme or which echo the story in some way.

Examples

Poem:

August Afternoon, by Marion Edey
In *A First Poetry Book*, published by Oxford University Press, 1979.

Song:

It's a Great Great Shame
No. 44 in *Every Colour Under the Sun*, published by Ward Lock Educational Co. Ltd, 1983.

Quiet reflection or prayer

For a universal, humanistic or multi-faith assembly:

Quiet reflection

The assembly leader says:

Why is power for one person – a dictator – a bad thing? (Pause) Let us be thankful that in this country we have shared power through the vote. (Pause) Think about how we can be fair in the classroom. (Pause) It is better to solve disagreements through discussion and negotiation than through violence and force.

Or for Christian schools:

Prayer

Let us pray.

Lord God,
We pray for all those who seek to protect democratic rights throughout the world. Bless our Circle Time and help us to settle our disagreements in peaceful ways.

Amen.

Chapter 10

The Careless Boy

Circle Time Ten

Teacher's Notes

Theme Ten: The value of **Value**

Circle Time Value: It is only if we come to **value our activities** that we live a rich and interesting life. It is only if we come to **value people** that we will learn to love and to be kind.

> Circle Time provides a forum in which the children can explore their own values and learn to value each other.

Circle Time Plan

This five-part lesson plan is only a guide. Teachers are likely to add to or amend the learning activities which are suggested and may sometimes wish to substitute their own. For any part of the session they may wish to allow more or less time than that suggested.

1 Introduce the theme   *3–6 minutes*

What is **value**? (To come to care for something or someone and find it/ them of worth.) How can we show that we value each other in Circle Time?

2 Vocabulary   *3–6 minutes*

The teacher ensures that the children understand the words given.

3 The story   *6 minutes*

The teacher shows the illustration and reads the story.

4 Talking about the story   *10–20 minutes*

The teacher uses some of the questions and discussion points given, stimulating the children to talk about the story/theme.

5 The Circle Time learning activity   *10–20 minutes*

The activities aim to help children to understand the importance of values and to think about their own. Some suggested activities could be used in follow-up lessons.

Total time   *30–60 minutes (approx.)*

1 ▮ INTRODUCE THE THEME

Key points

- Every human being is valuable. We must learn to treat everyone as a worthwhile person deserves to be treated.

- We value activities which we enjoy and which we can learn from – especially if we can become increasingly skillful.

- We value moral principles because we recognise their "goodness" – Being Fair, Being Honest, Being Kind.

2 ▮ VOCABULARY

Use your usual methods for introducing new words.

The difficult words in the story are:

careless	–	not taking care; not looking after something
creep	–	move quietly
slouched	–	walked in drooping, lazy manner
gratitude	–	thankfulness; appreciation of a favour
brooded	–	worried moodily
keen	–	enthusiastic
wobbled	–	shivered like jelly
admiring	–	looking up to; thinking well of; appreciative of quality
coma	–	unconscious state
fretting	–	worrying
progress	–	improving; move forward in skill or development

The colloquial words are:

clocked	–	noticed
nicked	–	stole
brat	–	annoying child
scoffed	–	made scornful remark
sussed	–	solved, worked out
buzz	–	intense satisfaction

3 THE STORY:

Careless Boy

Careless Boy

Mum droned on and on; nag, nag, nag. Said I was careless. Said I'd cracked the glass. I shrugged and went to watch the telly. She even came nagging about that.

"Keep it down," she said. "He's asleep."

My step-dad's on nights, but day or night we always had to creep round him.

"Here, make yourself useful," Mum said. "Take this to Gran's. She's out of milk again."

Gran's a tea junkie. Well, I was in no hurry. She'd just have to wait.

I called at Tug's. His Mum said he might be at the brook. On the way there I clocked a small kid with a lolly, still wrapped, so I nicked it. The brat yelled loud enough to wake the dead. I scarpered quick and scoffed it at Gran's.

"You took your time," she said, giving me a sour look.

There's gratitude, the old tea bag, I thought. Accidentally on purpose I knocked over her china cup; the one she keeps special for her tea.

"Now see what you've done!" she said, looking upset.

"I don't care," I said. "What's the matter with you? It's only a cup!"

"You don't care about anything, Max. That's your trouble," Gran said.

All the way home I brooded on Gran's words. The old nag-bag was right on this one. I didn't care about anything much, except, funny enough, I did care about not caring, if you see what I mean. It bothered me that I wasn't interested in anything. Not really. Even my stroppy step-dad was keen on football. The truth is, I was bored most of the time. I didn't care much about my family and they didn't care about me. They all look after number one. Sometimes I sussed that the other kids were bothered about things that left me cold. Like if we were all kept in at school because someone wouldn't own up. "It's not fair," they muttered to each other. Like it mattered. And they were all mega-upset when the class dog died. It was only a dog, but even Tug was upset about the dog.

Anyway, I was brooding on all this when I got back home. My step-dad was up by then. He gave me a mean look so I took myself off. I went to the garden shed where I practise my guitar. When I can be bothered that is. Fact is, with practice I could be good.

I hammered out several fast and angry riffs. When I looked up, I found I was staring out of the window, right into the face of the new boy next door. The little kid had climbed up on their side of the fence and was watching me. He grinned, showing a gap in his front teeth and gave me a thumbs up. I shot out, meaning to tell him to clear off, fast.

"That was brill," he said, before he wobbled and disappeared. I looked over the fence. He'd fallen off a big beach ball that he'd been balancing on and was in a heap on the ground, helpless with laughter. I couldn't help grinning myself. I propped my guitar against the fence and climbed over. The boy watched with admiration.

"You could be in the SAS," he said, which made me grin some more. I lifted my old guitar over the fence and showed him some fancy chords. I let him try, and even with his small hands, he did OK.

"Tom. Tea time," someone called from the house.

"Got to go," he said. "What's your name?"

"Max," I said.

"Well thanks, Max, that was cool. Wish I could play like that."

He raced off, and I climbed back over the fence.

After that, Tom and I often met up at the shed. Fact is, I liked having an admiring audience and I was getting better. Sometimes I climbed the fence and gave Tom another go. He loved that. One day his Mum was there. She smiled at me.

"I want to thank you, Max," she said. "Tom really enjoys your lessons. Look, have this towards some new music." She handed me a fiver.

"Thanks," I said, surprised.

We went on our bikes to buy the music. There's a steep hill down to the shops. Showing off I whizzed along, riding "no hands" for the last bit. At the music shop I stopped and looked back. Tom, grinning from ear to ear, was copying me. His arms were out like a plane. He wobbled a bit. What happened next was so awful, it sometimes replays in my head in slow motion. Tom's wheel hit a parked car and Tom was flung off his bike, cracking his head against the curb. I ran to him. I thought he was dead. His eyes were closed and he was very still. A crowd gathered and someone sent for an ambulance. I went with Tom to the hospital. His Mum arrived looking white and scared. It turned out that Tom was in a coma.

I was taken home. I didn't tell anyone about the "no hands", but I couldn't stop thinking about it. If only he hadn't copied me.

About a week later, Tom's Mum knocked at our door.

"Max," she said, "Tom's no better. We've tried just about every-thing to wake him up. The doctor thinks if you played to him on your guitar, it just might bring him round."

"I'll come right now," I said. I collected the guitar and she drove me to the hospital. I was jumpy to be there, fretting at every red light.

The kid's face was whiter than the pillow; his freckles dark against his white skin. I felt as though a sharp rock of pain was stuck in my chest.

I played my heart out on that old guitar. I played every day for a week – talking to Tom in between the music. On the eighth day his eyes flickered open. He looked at me and he smiled.

That was the start of Tom getting better. He never got com-pletely right. I mean, it took him longer to make progress on the guitar, but we never gave up. We practised in his house once he was home. It was great there. Tom's Mum even bought me a red Strat. I love that guitar, and with all the practising, I can even play Oasis stuff now. It's a great buzz when I first master a hard chord, or make my Strat sing with grief and joy. And I get that same buzz whenever Tom learns something. He gets it too. He looks up and grins his gap-tooth grin.

4 TALKING ABOUT THE STORY

Did the children understand?

- Why did Max have to creep round his Dad when he was on nights? What about when he was not on nights?

- Before he met Tom, what was the one thing that Max cared about?

- Why did Tom topple from his side of the fence?

- Where did Max and Tom practise before the accident? Where did they practise afterwards?

- Why did Max break Gran's cup on purpose?

- What things did Max value by the end of the story? (E.g. friendship with Tom; getting better at guitar; red Strat.)

Points for discussion

- What does it mean to value something?

- What do the children value?

- What do we value in Circle Time?

- What is wrong with not valuing anything at all?

5 THE CIRCLE TIME LEARNING ACTIVITY

1 Warm-up game

Go round the Circle: "I like _____" (E.g. chocolate, playing football, my dog.)
  In pairs the children find out some likes and dislikes of their partner. Go round the Circle: Each child gives one like and one dislike of their partner. e.g. "Mary likes her dog. She dislikes being cold."

2 Circle contribution

Explain that to value something is a bit different to liking it. Usually you do like it *and* consider that it has worth and merit too.
  Give some examples of things/people you value. (Include objects, principles, Circle Time, the children, a special book, a pet, the sea, etc.)
  Go round the Circle. Tell us two things you value.
  Go round the Circle. What/who makes *you* feel valued or valuable?

3 Circle discussion

Photocopy the Circle of Values for each child.
  Explain the Circle of Values.

(i)   Discuss what we value about ourselves and why we each need to be valued.

(ii)   Discuss what we value about other people (what values and qualities help us to value others).

(iii) What do we value in the Environment (in the natural world, in our classroom)?

(iv) What are the values of Circle Time? (E.g. Democracy means taking turns.)

(v)   Why do we value VALUING? (Makes life more interesting and worthwhile.)

4   Circle group work

The group make their own **Circle of Values** wall chart.

Have a large white card circle pasted onto a large coloured sheet of paper – to form a wall chart. (Alternatively the white circle could be tacked onto the background sheet in such a way that the Circle can be turned – in this case the words should be written **around** the circle rather than **across** the circle.) Let each child write one of their "valued" things, in the appropriate position on the card.

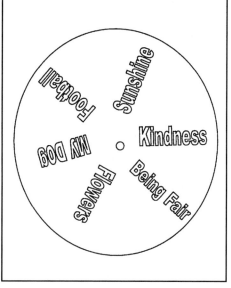

Static   Turning

The Careless Boy

Literacy Hour Ten

Teacher's Notes

Theme Ten: The value of **Value** in literature

Literacy Skills: Literature is full of values – the values of the
characters and of the themes of the stories.
Literature is also itself of great value (plays, stories,
books – all these enrich our lives). Literacy – being
able to read and write – is also of great practical
value. It is useful in many ways.

> **Literacy Hour provides a regular time in which to come to recognise all
> these valuable aspects of literacy and literature – to absorb, understand and
> treasure these.**

Literacy Hour Plan

This five-part lesson plan is only a guide. Teachers are likely to add to or amend the learning activities which are suggested and may sometimes wish to substitute their own. For any
part of the session they may wish to allow more or less time than that suggested.

1 Introduce the theme   *3–6 minutes*

How is literacy useful? Why is literature worthwhile?

2 Vocabulary   *3–6 minutes*

Can the children produce synonyms, antonyms and sentences for the
difficult words (which were covered in the Circle Time session)?

3 The story   *6 minutes*

This could be told or read by the children.

4 Talking about the story   *10–20 minutes*

The teacher uses some of the questions and discussion points given,
stimulating the children to talk about the story as a narrative. This helps
the children to develop a (literary) meta-language.

5 The Literacy Time learning activity   *10–20 minutes*

Some of the suggested "literacy" activities encourage group work as
a positive enhancement of the Circle Time skills and values. Some
suggested activities could be used in follow-up lessons.

| **Total time** | *30–60 minutes (approx.)* |

1 INTRODUCE THE THEME

Key points

- We have explored self values (e.g. self-esteem, self-expression), social values (empathy, kindness, friendship, cooperation etc.), environmental values (protection and appreciation of the environment and the natural world). We have seen the Circle Time Value of democracy. Now we can recognise the value of Value – of recognising that many things are of great worth!

- One area of great worth is Literature (e.g. stories **enhance/enrich** our lives – **intrinsic** value; being able to read and write is **useful – extrinsic** value).

---

2 VOCABULARY

Can you think of a word(s) that means the same as/the opposite to each of these? For each of the words, make up a sentence containing that word.

careless	gratitude
creep	brooded
slouched	wobbled
keen	SAS
admiring	coma
fretting	progress

3 THE STORY

With younger children – ask them to use their own words to tell the story (*The Careless Boy*) which they listened to in Circle Time. With older children, go round the class having the children (re-) read the story out loud. Alternatively, give the children time to (re-) read the story to themselves.

The Careless Boy

4 TALKING ABOUT THE STORY

Did the children understand?

- We saw Max change in this story. He comes to care. Does the main character in a story always change in some way?

- Max feels bad when Tom is in a coma. He finds that caring about someone can bring pain and worry. Why can "caring" be both hard/hurtful and have "value"?

Points for discussion

- What a person values can tell us something about that person. Give examples and ask the children for examples too. (E.g. a person who values kindness and hates cruelty is not likely to be a bully.)

- Are there things that we value in both Circle Time and Literacy Hour? (E.g. Clear communication. Group work.)

- What, for you, is the message of this story? (E.g. Be kind to be happy. Caring is good. Don't be cruel/mean.) The children should understand there is not just one correct answer.

5 THE LEARNING ACTIVITY

1   **Songs and Poems** (resources needed: poetry or song anthologies)

In pairs or small groups, find a poem or song which connects with the story. (It could be about caring/love; being cruel/mean; music; being ill, etc.) Ask some of the children to read out their chosen poem or song.

2   **Story discussion**

Consider some other stories (e.g. those recently read in class, shown on TV; or well-known fairy tales). Explore in what ways the situation/main character(s) have **changed** by the end of the stories.

3   **Individual activity**

In some stories the main character's situation changes. (E.g. Cinderella is no longer a poor, undervalued girl in an ordinary family. She becomes a Princess in the rich royal household.) In **other** stories, it is **part** of the story that an aspect of the character or situation of the protagonist changes (is transformed), as in "The Careless Boy". These are known as **transformation** stories. Write a transformation story of your own.

4   **Group activity**

A version of the story has been transformed into a play. This script can be read aloud in class. (Give each child a chance to read by **changing** the cast scene by scene. This allows for approximately 30 parts/children.) If teacher and children wish, the play could be (double-) cast (there are about 15 parts) and worked on and acted out as a class play.

The Careless Boy

A Play for Children in Two Acts by Mal Leicester

Cast

In order of appearance

Max	*The Careless Boy (Max is about eleven)*
The Dog	*A sheepdog*
Max's Mum	
Tom	*The new boy next door (Tom is about eight)*
Tom's Mum	
Gran	
Sparkly Sheep	*A magic sheep*
Snowball	*A sheep*
	Some other (non-speaking) sheep
Tug	*Max's mate at school*
Adam	
Jake	
Megan	
Little Kid	
Other non-speaking children if wished	
Doctor	
Nurse	
(The Chuckle Masters)	
NB	Max, Tom and Tug are boys' parts
	Max's Mum, Tom's Mum and Gran are girls' parts
	The Sparkly Sheep and Snowball and the dog can be boys or girls
	The Doctor can be boy or girl
	The other Sheep can be boys or girls
	14/15 parts plus **extra** non-speaking sheep and extra non-speaking children could be accommodated.

Summary

Max is the careless boy. He cares about nothing and no one, except, oddly, he cares about **not** caring because he recognises that this makes him different from the other children. The play is about how Max comes to care.

Act One

In Act One we see the uncaring, unkind Max being mean to a sheepdog, his grandma and another child Adam. However, almost by accident, through his guitar, he makes friends with Tom, the new boy next door.

Act Two

In Act Two Tom has a road accident and is in a coma. Max helps to bring Tom out of this by playing his guitar day and night at Tom's bedside in the hospital. Max finds he cares about Tom and that caring can be hard. The play ends with Tom back home, once more enjoying his guitar lessons with Max. They are both getting to be much better guitarists – something else that Max has come to value. He apologises to Adam. He is no longer uncaring and unkind.

The Careless Boy

A Play for Children in Two Acts by Mal Leicester

Act One

Scene One: At The Garden Shed

Max and his Mum are at one end of the stage.

There is a garden shed in the centre of the stage. (Optional if difficult!)

Just beyond the shed is a fence and at the far end of the stage there is a field (with sheep). The sheep Baa from time to time.

Max holds a guitar.

Mum	You are so careless, Max! Now look what you've done.
Max	What?
Mum	Trampled on my nice bluebells, that's what!
Max	What does it matter? They're only weeds, Mum. You see loads in the woods.
Mum	Yes, but I wanted some here. Not that you care about that! Anyway, practise in the shed. Dad's on nights and trying to sleep.
Exit Mum	
Max	Yeah. Mr Moan. I'll keep out of his way alright.
	Max goes to the shed and begins to practise on his guitar. (He then plays a recognisable, appropriate song. E.g. If I had a hammer or Imagine).
	A sheepdog appears on the stage from the direction of the field of sheep. It sniffs about. Max doesn't see the dog until it comes sniffing at the open door of the shed.
Max	Hey, clear off, dog. Scoot.
	Max puts down the guitar and comes out of the shed. He kicks at the dog, which cowers and tries to get away.
Max	I thought I told you to scoot (*Kick. Kick*). Clear out. Clear out.
	The sheep are watching this. They bleat in distress.
	A boy's head appears over the next door's fence. (Tom)
Tom	Hey. Don't do that! You'll hurt him.
	Max turns and the dog takes the chance to limp away, clearly hurt.
Max	Mind your own –
	Tom disappears with a wail. He has been balancing on a big ball and fallen off. He is laughing. Max looks over and can't help laughing too.
	Tom gets up, brushing himself down.
Tom	I heard you playing your guitar. That was fantastic! I wish I could play like that.

Max climbs over the fence and lifts over his guitar. He plays to his admiring audience.

Tom	You're really good.
Max	You must be the new kid next door, right? I'll show you some chords if you like.

Max gives Tom a short lesson – showing him some basic chords.

Tom's Mum calls from off the stage.

Tom's Mum	Tom. Dinner's ready.
Tom	I've got to go. That was cool. What's your name?
Max	Max
Tom	Well, thanks Max. See you.

Max climbs back over the fence and, as Tom runs off, Max's Mum comes back on stage.

Mum	Gran's out of milk again, Max. Take this would you? You know how much she likes her cuppa.
Max	I know how she's an old tea-bag! That's what I know. Anyway, I'm practising like you said.
Max's Mum	It won't take a minute.

Max shrugs and begins to play again.

Max's Mum	*(raising her voice above the guitar.)* Do as you're told, Max. Right now. Or I'll tell your father. You want another smacking, do you?

Max puts his guitar in the shed, snatches the milk and stamps off in a bad mood.

Max's Mum	*(looking after him)* He's always in a bad mood these days. Never wants to help anyone. The older he gets the worse he seems to be. Just like his Dad!

CURTAIN

The curtain closes leaving the front part of the stage empty. A chair and a table (with a cup and saucer) are quickly put in place, and Gran sits in the chair for Scene Two.

Scene Two: At Gran's House

Gran is sitting in her chair. A knock is heard from off-stage.

Gran	Come in, lad. It's open.

Max enters with the milk.

Gran	Your Mum just rang. She said you were on your way.
Max	Yeah.

He hands the milk to Gran.

Max	Here. Milk.
Gran	Thanks love. I'm dying for me cuppa.

She begins to get up with difficulty, but Max doesn't help Gran.

Gran	Want a cup?

Max	Not tea! You got any pop?
Gran	I'll see.
	She goes off-stage and shouts back to Max.
Gran	I'm out of pop, love. Forgot to get some. It's tea or nothing, I'm afraid.
Max	Mean old wrinkly.
	Max deliberately knocks Gran's cup to the floor. It breaks.
Max	Gran, I've broke your cup. It was an accident.
	Gran re-enters.
Gran	Oh no! My favourite cup. Why can't you be more careful?
	She begins to pick up the pieces with difficulty. Max watches, grinning.
Max	Why should I care? Anyway, its only a cup!
Gran	That's your trouble, Max. You don't care about anything!
Max	That's it! Forget the lecture. I'm off.
	Max walks towards the "door" and off the stage, and Gran exits (kitchen) side.
	Max stares out towards the audience.
Max	The old bat's right for once. I don't care about anything. All the other kids seem to. They care about who wins at football or even about that cat that was stuck up the tree. All sorts of daft things. But not me. I wish I did, really.
	He slouches off-stage.

CURTAIN

The curtain opens on a (simple) school playground for Scene Three.

Scene Three: The Playground

It is playtime at school. Some kids are playing together. Adam is on a bench reading a book. Max and Tug come swaggering by. They stop by the bench.

Max	Hey, Pig Face. What you reading?
Adam	*(Showing the book)* An adventure story. Not bad. Brill in fact.
Tug	Brill! Sounds like a brillo pad.
	Max and Tug laugh.
Max	Here. Let's have a look.
	Adam hands over the book reluctantly. Max opens it and begins to scrub it on the arm of the bench.
Max	Scrub the bench brillo pad.
Adam	Don't do that! It's my library book.
	Max tears out the page, scrunches it up and tosses it away. He is staring at Adam.
Max	Or what?
	He tears out another page.

Tug	Hey, leave the book Max.
	Max thrusts his face at Adam.
Max	You trying to pick a fight?
	Adam shakes his head, cowering back. Max bangs the book on Adam's head and then tosses the book onto the bench.
Tug	Come on, Max. Let's go.
Max	Yeah. He's too chicken to fight anyway.
Max	Listen, Cry Baby. You tell on me and I'll punch your head in.
	As Tug and Max walk to the front of the stage, Adam grabs his book and wipes his eyes. The curtain closes leaving Max and Tug at the front of the stage.
Tug	Sometimes you go too far, mate. If Adam tells Miss, you'll be in real trouble about that book.
Max	Na! He'll not go grassing. Too scared, right?

CURTAIN

Scene Four: At the Shed Again

	Max is giving Tom a lesson in the shed. The sheep are in the field beyond.
Max	You're getting much better.
Tom	Nowhere near as good as you, Max.
Max	I've got better myself through showing you, right?
	Tom's Mum appears.
Tom's Mum	Hi, you two. You must be Max. He loves your guitar lessons. I'm his Mum, by the way.
Max	Hi. He's got quite good now.
Tom's Mum	Thanks to you, Max.
Tom	Yeah. And I'm having a guitar of my own! Tomorrow. For my birthday.
Tom's Mum	He can't wait. Anyway, Tom wants to share some of his birthday money with you Max. For some guitar music for your practice.
	Tom's Mum hands Max some money.
Max	Hey, thanks! Both of you. I'll buy some today.
Tom's Mum	Anyway, Tom, you've got to come in now. You've got to go to the dentist, remember?
Tom	Oh no! I hate the dentist!
	They go off. Max strums quietly on his guitar.
Max	I seem to care about playing my guitar now I've got better at it. Maybe I can change after all.
	He carries on quietly strumming.
Snowball	Hey, Sparky, isn't that the mean bully who hurt our sheepdog?
Sparkly Sheep	Yes, Snowball. That's the boy.

Snowball	Why did he do it? Lucy never harmed anyone in her life. She's even gentle with us!
Sparkly Sheep	He was feeling mean and angry. It makes him quite a cruel boy.
Snowball	Well you mended Lucy's leg, Sparky. It must be great to be a magic sheep! I wish I had those magic sparks.
Sparkly Sheep	You're fine as you are, Snowball. You're kind. That's the most important thing. Not like the boy!
Snowball	Hey, I've had an idea. Why don't you magic him to be kind?
Sparkly Sheep	I can't do that Snowball. Even magic can't do that. Only caring about people makes you kind.
	All the sheep sing a song about kindness. (E.g. Seeds of Kindness)
	The other sheep wander off the stage, leaving Sparky. The sparkling sheep's sparkles grow noticeably brighter.
Sparkly Sheep	By the glinting of my sparks
	Something tells me Max Parks
	Wants to change if change he dare
	Will careless boy yet come to care?

CURTAIN

INTERVAL

Act Two

Scene One: At The Garden Shed

	Max is at the front of the stage. He is strumming on his guitar. His playing is noticeably better. There is a knock from the side. Max's Mum enters with Tom's Mum. Tom's Mum looks pale and worried.
Max's Mum	Mrs Piper wants to speak to you, Max.
Max	Hi, Mrs Piper. Is it about Tom? I've not seen him for ages.
	Mrs Piper begins to cry. Max's Mum pats her shoulder.
Max	Hey. Are you OK? What's up?
Tom's Mum	It's Tom. He's had an accident.
	She continues to cry.
Max	An accident!
	Max's Mum nods
Max's Mum	He was hit by a car, Max.
Tom's Mum	He's been badly hurt. He's been in the hospital in a coma since Tuesday.
	She cries a bit more and Max watches helplessly but looking concerned.
Max	Can't they do something? The doctors?

Tom's Mum	They've tried everything. I've told them about you. We're desperate Max. Will you help?
Max	Me?
Tom's Mum	The doctor thinks Tom might come out of the coma if you play to him. You know how he loves your playing. Will you come to the hospital? It's worth a try. Please.
Max	Of course I will.
	He picks up his guitar.
Max	Let's go. Now! Right?
	Max and Tom's Mum hurry off. Max's Mum follows more slowly, shaking her head sadly.
	From off the stage we hear:
Snowball	Oh dear. Oh dear. Have you heard, Sparky? That nice little kid is in a coma. I do hope he'll be OK.
Sparkly Sheep	Dangerous things, those cars, Snowball.
Snowball	Sparky, could you use your magic to –
Sparkly Sheep	No. No, Snowball. Not at this distance I can't. The hospital's too far away. It's up to the doctors now. To make Tom better. If they can.
	All the sheep go Baa.

Scene Two: The Hospital

	Tom is pale and unconscious in his hospital bed. A white-coated doctor is feeling his pulse and checking the monitors, etc.
Doctor	I'm afraid there's no change, Mrs Piper.
Tom's Mum	Well, Doctor, this is Max. Tom's friend. With his guitar.
Doctor	Ah yes! Splendid. Well, do your best, young man. Play the tunes that Tom knows best.
	He exits.
Tom's Mum	Come and sit here, Max.
	Max sits on a chair and immediately begins to play on his guitar.
	Tom's Mum kisses Tom's forehead.
	A nurse comes and checks Tom.
	Max continues to play.
	The lights fade.
	The music gradually fades too.
	After a few moments the lights brighten. Max and Tom's Mum are still at the bedside. The doctor comes in and does his checks.
Doctor	Still no change. And you're here again, Max, with your guitar.
Tom's Mum	He's played all day for three long days doctor. Played and played tirelessly. I'm beginning to lose hope.
	She sounds very sad.

Max	Don't give up, Mrs Piper. It could be today he wakes up. I've a feeling he's hearing me now.
Doctor	Try playing some chords you were teaching him last, Max.
Max	You mean the last lesson before the accident, right?
Doctor	It's worth a try.
	He exits as Max starts to strum chords.
Max	I've had an idea, Mrs Piper. Tom really liked this song. It was the first one he heard me play. He said it was fantastic.
	Max plays (If I had a hammer) and Tom begins to stir. He opens his eyes as the song comes to an end.
Tom's Mum	Tom! Honey!
	She kisses him gently.
Tom's Mum	Max, ring for the doctor, my dear.
	Tom smiles at Max.
Tom	Hi, mate. That was fantastic.
	Max and Tom's Mum laugh. They are both clearly excited.
	The doctor comes in.
Doctor (to Tom)	Well, well, young man. Back in the land of the living. Splendid!
CURTAIN	
	The Chuckle Masters are at the front of the stage, in front of the curtain, perhaps dressed as clowns.
Chuckle Master One	Well, here we are at the hospital, Chuckle. I like doing these visits to cheer up the children.
Chuckle Master Two	*(He chuckles)* The nurses call us The Chuckle Masters, did you know?
Chuckle Master One	Yeah. Lets tell some of our favourite jokes.
	They walk to the other end of the stage.
	The Chuckle Masters speak out to the audience.
Chuckle Master One	Hallo children. We've got some good jokes for you today.
	The Chuckle Masters tell their jokes. At the end they wave to the audience as they exit, saying:
Chuckle Master One	Bye for now, boys and girls.
Chuckle Master Two	Get well soon. Bye.
NB	They could throw sweets to the audience.

Scene Three: At Tom's House

	Tom is on a sofa, convalescing. Max is sitting with him, showing him some difficult chords on the guitar.
Max	You're doing really well, mate. You can play some quite hard riffs now.
Tom	And you can even do Oasis stuff!
Max	Yeah. I enjoy that.

Tom's Mum comes in with some drinks.

Tom's Mum	Here you are you two. Some drinks. And your tablets, Tom.

Tom takes his tablets.

Tom's Mum — He's getting much better, Max. And the guitar practice helps a lot. It's real nice of you to come everyday like this.

Max — Oh, I enjoy it, Mrs Piper.

Tom's Mum — I've a thank-you gift, Max. For all you've done.

Tom's Mum picks up a big parcel and hands it to Max.

Max opens it.

It is a red Stratocaster guitar. Tom and his Mum are smiling.

Max — Wow! Oh wow! A red Strat!

His voice is awed, and he strokes the guitar and strums it.

Max — Just hear that tone! Thanks a million. It's a treasure.

Tom — Isn't it great? You deserve it, too, mate. Mum says I might still be in that coma if it wasn't for you.

A knock on the door is heard.

Tom's Mum goes to answer it and comes back with other children. Two should be Tom's size and one, bigger, is Adam, whom Max bullied at school.

Tom's Mum — More friends to see you, Tom.

The two little kids hand a basket of fruit to Tom.

Little Kid — Our Mum sent this fruit, Tom. She said you're well enough for visitors now.

Tom — Yeah. Tell her thanks.

Adam — The big class at school all signed this Get-Well card for you.

He hands the envelope to Tom, who opens the card and adds it to others on the table by his sofa.

Adam — And this is from my Mum. A book about musical instruments.

Tom — Great! Tell her thanks.

The little kids look at the book with Tom, talking quietly about it. Adam is near Max's chair.

Max — Hey, look Adam, I'm sorry I was mean to you, OK?

Adam — OK. I guess.

Max — Look, I'm different now. I'll not bully you again.

Adam — Really! Promise?

Max — I promise. In fact, I'm saving up to buy you the book I tore up in the playground.

They shake hands.

Adam — You've changed, Max.

Max — Yeah.

Adam — You're kind and friendly now.

Max	And I'm happy too.
	There's another knock on the door.
Tom's Mum	More visitors! They mustn't stay too long though, Tom. I don't want you tired out.
	She goes out and returns, followed by all the rest of the cast – including The Chuckle Masters.
Tom	Let's have one more song before they all leave, Max. How about: *If I had a hammer?* (*i.e. the song should be Tom's favourite one, the "fantastic" one that brought him out of the coma*).
	*It could be a song everyone joins in with – **cast and audience**. The Chuckle Masters could encourage the audience.*
	At the end of the song the curtain closes and opens again for the cast to take their bow.

END

The Careless Boy
Assembly

Theme: Caring/Valuing

Introduction

The assembly leader introduces the theme. When we care about someone we value their well-being and will always help and support them. When we value an activity (e.g. playing the guitar, or playing football, or painting a picture) we will try hard to do it as well as we can and practise to improve. Caring therefore gives us a more interesting life and helps us to be who we are and to get better at what we do and how we behave.

Story

Assembly leader

Our story today is about Max – a boy who learns to care.

The assembly leader or a child reads the story – *The Careless Boy*.

Poem or Song

You can choose a poem or a song, or both. Alternatively, you can have a child (or children) read the poems they chose or wrote in class and have one of the songs that were chosen. Select poems and songs which are relevant to the theme or which echo the story in some way.

Examples

Poem:

Children
In *The Poetry Book*, published by Dolphin, 1996.

Song:

O Jesus We are Well and Strong
No. 40 in *Someone's Singing Lord*, published by A&C Black, 2002.

Quiet reflection or prayer

For a universal, humanistic or multi-faith assembly:

Quiet reflection

The assembly leader says:

Think about the people who care for you and feel grateful to them. (Pause) Think about those you care about and resolve to be helpful to them. (Pause) Think of the friendless and about how you might help them. (Pause) Now take a moment to think about your skills. What are you good at? How can you become even more skillful?

Or for Christian schools:

Prayer

Let us pray.

Dear God,
Thank you for the people who care for us. Help us to be more caring ourselves. Thank you for giving us the capacity to care.

Amen.